MARY WELLS

Mary Wells
1906
M<small>ONTANA</small>

MARY WELLS

JAMES A. FRANKS

WILD GOOSE PRESS
Santa Cruz, California

A percentage of the royalties from this book will
go to the Fort Belknap Reservation in Montana.

The cover painting of St. Peter's Mission, Cascade,
Montana, was painted by Mary Wells in 1890,
when she was 12 years old.

JULY 23, 1895 — ST. PETER'S MISSION

Fire broke out in the washhouse at about
10 A.M. Blankets and comforts near the chimney in
the upper room were found smouldering. Mary Wells
was married to Mr. Gump. They were married in
Church but had breakfast here.

—The Bird Tail
Sister Genevieve McBride. O.S.U.

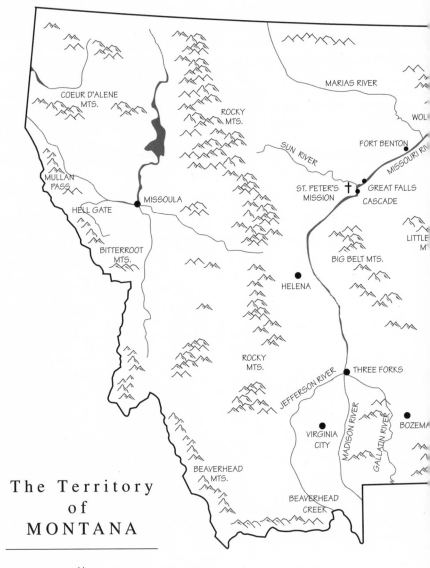

COEUR D'ALENE MTS.

ROCKY MTS.

MARIAS RIVER

WOL

FORT BENTON

SUN RIVER

MISSOURI RIV

MULLAN PASS

ST. PETER'S MISSION

GREAT FALLS

CASCADE

HELL GATE

MISSOULA

LITTLE M

BITTERROOT MTS.

BIG BELT MTS.

HELENA

ROCKY MTS.

THREE FORKS

JEFFERSON RIVER

MADISON RIVER

GALLATIN RIVER

BOZEMA

VIRGINIA CITY

BEAVERHEAD MTS.

The Territory
of
MONTANA

BEAVERHEAD CREEK

N

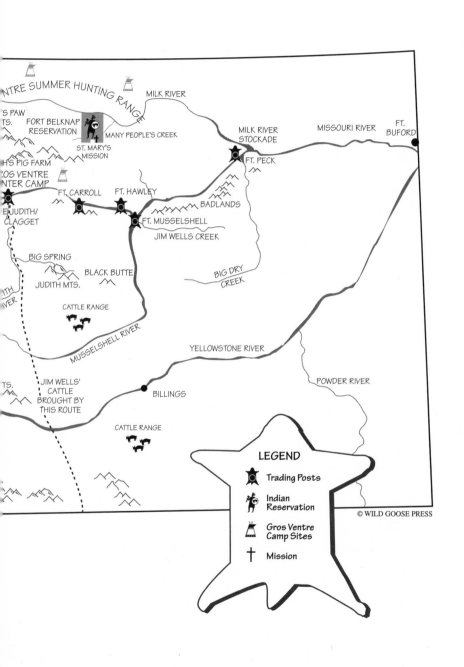

NTRE SUMMER HUNTING RANGE

MILK RIVER

'S PAW
TS.

FORT BELKNAP
RESERVATION

MANY PEOPLE'S CREEK

MILK RIVER
STOCKADE

MISSOURI RIVER

FT.
BUFORD

ST. MARY'S
MISSION

H'S PIG FARM

OS VENTRE
NTER CAMP

FT. PECK

E JUDITH/
CLAGGET

FT. CARROLL

FT. HAWLEY

FT. MUSSELSHELL

BADLANDS

JIM WELLS CREEK

ITH
VER

BIG SPRING

JUDITH MTS.

BLACK BUTTE

BIG DRY
CREEK

CATTLE RANGE

MUSSELSHELL RIVER

YELLOWSTONE RIVER

POWDER RIVER

TS.

JIM WELLS'
CATTLE
BROUGHT BY
THIS ROUTE

BILLINGS

CATTLE RANGE

LEGEND

Trading Posts

Indian
Reservation

© WILD GOOSE PRESS

Gros Ventre
Camp Sites

✝ Mission

PREFACE

IN DOING THE RESEARCH for my earlier book, *James Wells of Montana*, a tremendous amount of material surfaced regarding my grandmother, Mary Wells. Much of her story was derived from the Montana Historical Societies' archives in Helena, where her letters and the letters of her brothers and sister in correspondence with Senator T.C. Power and his brother John had been preserved. The details were further corroborated by information gathered from the Ursuline Center in Great Falls and the Gros Ventre reservation in Fort Belknap, Montana. Many of the facts pertaining to Mary Wells' later years were shared with me by my grandfather Joseph Gump, who married her at St. Peter's Mission on July 23, 1895.

My knowledge of the role of the Missions was obtained through personal interviews of Sister Genevieve McBride in 1983, before she died. Her book, *The Bird Tail*, pertains to daily life at St. Peter's Mission from its inception until it was destroyed by fire. *Jesuits in Montana*, by Wilfred Schoenberg, S.J., also provides great detail on the development of the Mission.

One of my greatest experiences in the last 20 years has been having the privilege to work with the Gros Ventre Indians at the reservation. They allowed me to interview them and gain in-depth information of their tribal history.

I hope this book will raise the question, "How do we show respect for and preserve all cultures and traditions which are part of the fabric of this nation?" If these should be destroyed, then we are a people without roots or heritage.

As for my method of composing Mary Wells, I have taken obvious liberties with dialogue, however, the names of all places and the events reported in the life of Mary Wells are authentic, as are the names of the principal characters.

ACKNOWLEDGMENTS

I am very grateful to the Ursuline Convent at Great Falls, to Joel Overholser in Ft. Benton, to the Montana Historical Society in Helena, and once again to Truby Stiffarm at the Fort Belknap Reservation in Montana for their contributions and support with this book.

MARY WELLS

INTRODUCTION

ALTHOUGH *MARY WELLS* stands on its own, my previous work, *James Wells of Montana*, sets the stage for Mary's story. The legacy of and decisions made by James Wells, Mary's father, stand silently behind the pages of this book.

Mary's story takes place from 1878 to 1937 starting on the plains of the Montana territory which is a vast area comprising two geographically distinct regions. The western part is characterized by magnificent mountain ranges running north and south and the eastern part is an almost endless high plateau referred to as the Great Plains. The Rocky Mountains divide the areas, west from east. Two great rivers rise from this range, the Missouri (Big River) on the north and the Yellowstone (Elk River) on the south. They run north then eastward, creating three parallel strips across the plains.

The A'a'ninin (pronounced Ah-Ahn-Ne-Nin) were one of numerous Indian tribes who roamed the Montana plains. Their name, White Clay People, derived from the white clay residue which would cover their bodies while making pottery. This skill was a rare one among the Plains Indians. The A'a'ninin, as all tribes of Montana, followed the buffalo herds who provided them with everything necessary to sustain life: food, shelter, clothing, even bone and sinew as tools. At one time, 80 million buffalo migrated across the Montana plains. By the time this story takes place, that number had been reduced to mere thousands. As the buffalo were disappearing, the Indians, too, were vanishing. In 1835, the A'a'ninin were ten thousand; by the 1880's they numbered fewer than two thousand. The A'a'ninin were called Gros Ventre (pronounced Grow Von) by the French.

Montana Indians had a long history of contact with white traders. The first white men to come to Montana were French, coming through Canada. They were followed by American traders. They came seeking beaver, buffalo, fox and wolf furs, all of which were stylish in Europe and the Eastern states. The river was their avenue of trade, being the fastest means of moving goods to and from Montana. As minerals were discovered and the need for farming and cattle land increased, white men found the Indians to be an impediment.

During the 1850s, just before the mining rushes that overwhelmed the area, the Indian tribes signed their first treaties with the federal government. Many treaties were made but none were ever kept. The U.S. Government assigned vast tracts of land to the Indians, only to take it as the whites demand for land grew.

By the mid-1870's, the Gros Ventre had been pushed completely north of the Missouri River. Their lush grasslands in the Judith basin were opened to stockmen. To the Indians, it meant the narrowing of their horizons to the borders of reservations and a deepening dependence upon the federal government, an indifferent Congress, and a corrupt Indian

Bureau that failed to provide the food and annuities promised by law.

The Congress of the United States made no law respecting the establishment of religion or curtailing the free exercise thereof. Yet, the Indians were forbidden to practice their religion on or off the reservations. Along with the eradication of the buffalo, the refusal of religious freedom was a significant tool used to undermine the identity of the Indians.

Each church was given a reservation by the government. Rather than converting the "pagans" to one religion, the Indian nations were further divided into Catholics, Methodists, and Quakers. The churches set up mission schools, forcing the Indian children to leave home and be educated away from their families and traditions.

It was in this period that Mary Wells was born.

CHAPTER ONE

ON SEPTEMBER 12, 1878, a daughter was born to a trader at the Judith River. She was named Mary Wells. The trader was James Wells and his wife, Maggie, was a Gros Ventre.

Their's was an unlikely union at a difficult time in the history of the Indian and the white man. James had come to Montana in 1860 with his brother John. They were enterprising young men, seeking opportunity.

One winter while on a fur-trapping expedition James fell deathly ill. Fearing for James' life, John took him to the nearest Indian encampment. These were the Gros Ventre (pronounced Grow Von), also known as the A'a'ninin (pronounced Ah-Ahn-Ne-Nin), that had a reputation of being friendly towards whites. He approached with trepidation because the methods white trappers used to secure the hides of wolves were threatening to the Indian's existence.

Much to his relief, this was a band that he and his brother had traded with at an earlier time. The Gros Ventre were willing to care for James. John departed for Fort Benton leaving much of his supplies and hides in payment for the necessary care of his brother. His leaving haunted him. He wondered if he'd ever see James again.

James lay delirious for many days, ministered to by the gentle hands of the chief's daughter. As life began to re-enter his body, he rested in the care of this lovely young Indian woman. He felt that she was willing him to live, bolstering him with her prayers and entreaties to the Great Spirit. Although her words were foreign to his ears, they soothed him. He began to question his preconceived notions, instilled in him by fellow whites, about the dearth of spirituality in these people. They did not turn him away in his time of need. Comforted by her prayers, he felt more unified in body, mind, and soul than he had ever felt in his life. He knew that the one whom the Indians called "Great Spirit" was also his God.

James began a one-sided conversation with his lovely caretaker. Her eyes were filled with a quiet intelligence that seemed beyond her years, and her hands were healing and cool on his feverish head. He thanked her, praised her beauty, told her tales of his life's journey, and before he knew it he was expressing his heartfelt love for this woman and how inspired he was by her ways.

James had made an assumption while listening to her prayers and looking into her eyes. He assumed that she didn't understand him, because he did not understand her words. What a shock it was to find out that she had been educated in Fort Benton and spoke English. This small infraction on his part, of assuming that she did not understand English, was an example of how his culture continually misunderstood Indians. It was becoming very hard for him to comprehend why whites mistrusted the Indians, when here they were saving his life and sharing what little they had with him.

His heart was troubled when he contemplated the heavy-handed way white men were dealing with the Indians: trying to stamp them out, trying to "take the Indian out of them" by proselytizing and denying the reality of their God. They were a people joined with the very heart of Montana. Those who had once roamed the land freely were being methodically corraled into tight corners called "reservations." They were a people united with nature, and tied to the buffalo for their very existence. It was the buffalo who provided them with clothing, shelter, food, and utensils. The white man's strategy was to exterminate the creatures on whom the Indians depended for sustenance. By eliminating their food source, they drew the circle smaller, pulling the rope ever more steadily into a tightening noose.

It took months before James regained his strength and the ability to return to his brother in Fort Benton. Making the appropriate observances, he requested Maggie in marriage, promising he would care for her with his life's breath. Maggie's father did not oppose the engagement but believed that when James left the encampment he would grow fickle, taking on the white man's ways. He suspected James would never return to marry his daughter. When James actually did return a couple of months later, he brought many gifts for Maggie's father and the tribe. He was willing to be married in the tradition of the Gros Ventre and also brought with him a Catholic priest, since Maggie had converted to Catholicism at Fort Benton while being educated. James himself was not a Catholic.

Unlike other white men who took Indian brides, James showed Maggie great respect. He was very committed to her, marrying Maggie because he loved her and wanted to care for her. Their bond grew. They were not only husband and wife, but he sought her counsel in trading with Indians from the many different tribes.

James proved his ability as a trader and proprietor while running posts for T.C. Power. Mr. Power was a wealthy merchant bringing goods up the Missouri River which were dispersed to the many trading posts in the territory. James went to T.C. Power to propose his theory. He believed that if a trading post was established at the Judith Basin, where the Judith and Missouri rivers intersect, this trading post could receive supplies a month earlier in the spring and a month later in the fall. Supplies could then be brought overland from the Judith Basin to Helena. James wanted to be a full partner in this endeavor. T.C. Power agreed and a partnership was formed.

When the trading post was started, James could see the potential for establishing a cattle ranch at the Judith. He felt that cattle were the future for Montana's economy. The land around the Basin was well-protected and ideal for this endeavor. James went to Texas to buy stock.

James made it back to the Judith in time for the birth of their third child. Maggie had hoped that this child would be a girl. Her hopes were fulfilled. She wanted a daughter to whom she could pass on the traditions that she had received from her mother. She felt the Indian ways were being torn from her people. The traditions must live on! Her hopes of preserving them were with her daughter.

Blue Sky, a friend to James and Maggie for many years and a Gros Ventre herself, was there for the delivery. She had been with the family for the traditional birth of all of their children.

One of the strengths of James and Maggie's marriage was his acceptance of her practices and traditions surrounding birthing. Although he did not understand many of them, he had great respect for Maggie, Blue Sky, and their people's ways. He felt very much a part of the birth. If any questions arose, Maggie and Blue Sky answered them in detail. These were not merely rules but were traditions laden with great meaning, reminding them of their participation in, rather than rule over, life.

During the pregnancy, Maggie was only to have good thoughts and look at pleasant and familiar things that would not have any ill-effects on the unborn child. Maggie was never to look upon a corpse or she might have a still-born baby. Blue Sky had taken good care of Maggie and had not let her work because it was known if you worked hard, you had a hard delivery. Maggie was not allowed to cook, because the heat from the fire makes the after birth sticky and hard to come out.

Maggie was required to wear a robe on her back so the sun couldn't spoil her milk. When Maggie was in bed, if she wanted to change sides, she had always to sit up first then lie down again on the other side. She must not simply roll over. If she did, Gros Ventre tradition said the cord would wrap around the infant's neck and there would be a stillbirth. When she entered or left a lodge or cabin, she must move through the door quickly. If she stood in the door the baby wouldn't come quickly. And, she must never back into a lodge as this would make the baby come out the wrong way.

Jim was required to move out of the house for the last month of the pregnancy. He had done this for the last two births. This was because the couple must absolutely restrain from intimate relations or the child would be born with a heavy grease-like cover and could suffocate or have bad lungs.

Maggie followed each of these traditions and many more. When it was time for the birth, she bore the pain and never let a noise out as the child could only hear good sounds and not screams of pain. Also, the screams of pain could drive the baby back and make for a long delivery.

The umbilical cord was always cut about six inches long so the child would not bleed to death and when the umbilical cord fell off, it could be put into the medicine bag. The cord was part of the owner's body, so when it dropped in four or five days it was placed in a small fancy buckskin pouch filled with sweet grass and it was hung around the baby's neck. This pouch would be worn into adulthood and many were buried with their pouches.

This baby was a healthy child and came into the world with a very loud and strong voice. Immediately upon the birth, Blue Sky took the afterbirth and disposed of it in a secret place in the branches of a high tree so the baby would not be afflicted with sores.

Maggie was given a special root to make her milk come but the baby was not put on the breast immediately. Blue Sky had to suck and spit out the first milk until it was the right blue color, then the baby could nurse.

Maggie's tribe was slowly being pushed out of its hunting area. A reservation had been established called "Fort Belknap," but the tribe still occupied land along the Milk River, on the east side of the Missouri, extending as far as the Cypress Mountains. From this line to the Marias River stretched a beautiful level country which was covered with grass and well adapted to buffalo. In this area the Gros Ventre could be found year around, in the winter along the banks of the Milk River or the Judith River where wood was plentiful, and in the summer on the Plains where buffalo chips could be used as fuel. The Gros Ventre were not native to this area but at this time most could be found there.

The U.S. Government believed that by destroying the Great Buffalo herds they could control the Indians. As all white men knew, this day of destruction of the buffalo was rapidly approaching; first with the completion of the Union Pacific railroad in 1869, which split the Northern and Southern buffalo herds; and second, with the presence of increasing numbers of white commercial hunters, who were armed with long range repeating rifles. The real end of the great herd was under way by 1876. This slaughter increased each year and the United States government's intention was being accomplished.

The Judith trading post, however, was thriving, not only as a port for freight in early spring and late fall, but also as a ranch. All one had to do was walk out of the trading post door to see hay being stacked, new fencing and corrals going up all over, and the many grazing cattle which Jim himself had driven up from Texas. For the last two years the ice on the Missouri had broken early and the winters had been mild, so the herd was growing fast. And with the Army's demand for beef always present, James Wells was making money.

Every spring when the ice breaking came, everyone went down to the Missouri to watch. It was a great excitement to all. The roar and crash of the ice-fields could be heard for a great distance. Great floes of ice rushed by, heading up in huge masses as they swept down river with a furious current. All the lowlands were inundated with water. Far in shore was also covered with huge blocks of ice that the force of the water had thrown, like a little river up on land. The water would rise ten to fifteen feet in just minutes if an ice dam formed down river. Then it would break and the water would rush by, dropping its level as fast as it had risen.

The real joy was that this ice-breaking signaled the coming of spring. The arrival of boats with fresh supplies would soon follow.

In the summer of 1878, Jim made many trips to Fort Benton, which was becoming a big city. It now had a population of about 500. On one of his trips to Fort Benton, Jim made an appointment with a doctor to check on his cough. The cough had come the winter he was trapping furs, the winter he met Maggie. Consumption was the diagnosis he received last year on a trip down the Missouri River to Florida with his family. The consumption had progressed to a stage that was threatening his life and the doctor now informed him that he did not have long to live. Having known the severity of his illness, the news was not a surprise to Jim.

An hour later Jim was meeting with T. C. Power. Jim had a problem that needed to be solved. Since Jim's wife was a Gros Ventre, it was crucial that he plan carefully for her and his children's future. As an Indian, Maggie could not own property—even though she was his wife and he was a wealthy man. His children would be considered half-breeds and mother and children could be sent to reservations. Having given the matter serious thought, Jim proposed that T.C. Power be trustee for Jim's estate so that Maggie and their children would be properly taken care of. Jim told T.C. Power, as he signed the documents, that on paper T.C. had full power over everything that Jim owned. In truth, the money was Maggie's, but they both knew the law. As his partner, Jim requested that T.C. Power take care of Maggie and the children. Jim planned to purchase a home in Fort Benton for Maggie; and he wanted his children to receive an education. His vision was that they would continue to live as well as they lived now, which was easily possible given the size of his estate.

That night Jim explained the trustee agreement to Maggie. No matter what Jim told her, she knew the prejudicial way she had been treated in school in Fort Benton. She would still be treated that way if it wasn't for Jim. She felt very blessed to have a white husband who loved and respected her. Maggie was worried that Jim's protective care of her and their children would disappear.

The time came that Maggie feared. Jim told her that he wanted to sell his interest in the Judith and retire to Fort Benton. He felt that his health was going fast, and he wanted the family settled before anything happened to him. Maggie held back tears but understood. She knew that Jim was dying and dreaded what might befall her and their children.

Jim met with his men. He was certain that the Judith was established and would go on, so their jobs would be safe. Jim sent word to T.C. Power asking whether he knew anyone who wanted to buy his interest.

In June, Jim was contacted by Mr. Norris who would buy out his interest, continue to run the ranch, and keep the trading post going. A price was agreed upon and the papers were signed; the transfer would take place on July 1, 1884. The ground beneath Maggie began to slip away.

Jim and Maggie located a house in Fort Benton and the purchase was put into the transaction of the sale of the Judith. The house was near old Fort Benton and had four bedrooms and a porch that ran all the way around the house. Mary's room was upstairs and had a beautiful willow tree in front of the window.

Maggie had a strong belief that her children must understand both the native American and the white ways. She knew that her children couldn't survive as Indians in this white world but somehow they must carry on their heritage. The children would spend time in the summer with her tribe. The boys would learn from Capture, her father, who was a chief among their band. Mary was Maggie's to educate. Even from her birth, Mary was her father's favorite and when possible she would follow him around the Judith.

Maggie wanted Mary to understand the healing properties of plants, such as willow bark for pain and headache, bark of black locust as an emetic, wild gentian for stomach ailments, hazel bark poultice for ulcers, Indian turnip as a decoction for coughs and intermittent fevers (she made this for Jim's cough), May apple as a cathartic, milkweed as a decoction for dysentery, dropsy and asthma, moss from shell bark in an infusion for catarrhs and asthma, and a decoction of inner birch bark for coughs, colds and pulmonary diseases. Mary would have to learn how to use oak bark, pipsissewa, prickly ash, puccoon, rushes, pine, wild cucumber, and wild ginger, all of the many things that the Gros Ventre used to maintain good health.

As Jim's health continued to decline, he learned that they were trying to open a girls' school at St. Peter's. Jim wanted Mary to go to school at St. Peter's as soon as the girls' school opened, because he felt that if anything happened to him she would be safe there and would be treated well by the Ursuline nuns.

CHAPTER TWO

IN THE FALL, three of the Wells children were at St. Peter's Mission schools—Lee Roy, William, and Mary.

Mary soon met Miss Mary Fields, a very robust and friendly black woman. Although short, Miss Fields weighed over 200 pounds. Mary had not seen any black people since the family trip to Florida. Miss Fields took an instant liking to Mary. She told Mary, "Us Mary's must stick together," and they did. When Mary wasn't doing her mission duties, you could find her following Miss Fields, or "Black Mary" as everyone called her, except the children who had to call her Miss Fields.

Miss Fields had been born into slavery in Tennessee in 1832 into the Dunne family. The daughter of the Dunnes was Dolly Dunne, who became Mother Amadeus Dunne, who led the first Ursuline nuns to St. Peter's Mission in 1884. During that first year, Mother Amadeus had become very sick and had sent for Miss Fields to come and take care of her. With Miss Fields' help, Mother Amadeus recovered, and then she asked Miss Fields to stay and help the Ursulines at St. Peter's Mission. The only thing Mother Amadeus asked of Miss Fields was that she stop

smoking her cigars and her pipe. Miss Fields told Mother
Amadeus, "You want me, you take my cigars and my pipe." So
Miss Fields was allowed to smoke and was also known to go to
the town of Cascade now and then for a few drinks.

Because Mary came from a prosperous and respected family,
she and her brothers were treated very well their first autumn
at the Mission. But one day she mentioned to one of the nuns
that she had spent a few summers in a teepee with her mother's
people out on the plains. The nun said, "I'll pretend you never
said that." Mary was confused and sad.

That Christmas the children returned home and found their
father very ill. Once a man who could never sit still, James Wells
was barely able to move from a chair in the living room of his
house in Fort Benton. Mary was shocked to see her father so
gaunt and pale. She recited the Lord's Prayer, the Five Great
Truths, the Ten Commandments of God, and the Seven
Sacraments to cheer him up, and he laughed and asked if she
knew what any of it meant. Mary laughed too and said, "Not
all of it."

But by mid-January 1885 when the children were to return
to St. Peter's, Jim sent word that his children wouldn't be
returning for a while. Jim went into a coma on February 1, 1885,
and on February 11 he died with his family surrounding him.
Mary never left her father's side.

Lee Roy and William had made their father a coffin. Maggie
and Mary cleaned and prepared Jim and put him in his suit,
then placed him in the coffin. Lee Roy nailed down the lid, and
the family carried the coffin out to the wagon. The family drove
the wagon about five miles down the Missouri River. Mary
Wells never took her hand from the coffin. The family found a
meadow that wasn't covered by snow where the boys dug a
grave into which the family placed Jim's coffin. The finality of

the situation was becoming very clear to Maggie. She now realized the great changes that would befall her family. Little Mary Wells said all her prayers for her father with the fervency that only a child could muster. It was the first time her young mind could not distinguish between the traditional prayers taught to her by her mother and those Christian prayers taught to her by the missionaries. The grave was covered first with dirt and then with rocks.

The children all said their good-byes, after which the family returned to Fort Benton. Maggie told Mary that her father's hand would always be in hers.

The *River Press* reported the following:

February 11,1885
Death of James Wells

We are called upon to chronicle the death of one of our most esteemed and respected citizens. James Wells passed away this morning at 6 o'clock after a long and painful sickness. His death was not unexpected, as for the past year no hopes have been entertained for his recovery, although until within a short time he had been buoyed up with the idea that he would yet recover. For several weeks he had been confined to his house. The following particulars relative to Mr. Wells were furnished by Mr. John W. Power [brother of T.C. Power] and others who have known him long and intimately. He was born in Indiana about 1840 and was therefore about 45 years of age. When he came west we could not learn, but he was in California and Oregon in early years and came to Montana in 1865 or 66. In 1868 he had a trading post on Milk River, about twenty miles above old Fort Browning. The following year he entered into the employ of T.C. Power and Bro. and served them in different capacities until the winter of 1874, when they established a post on Milk River, near the Black Butte.

*Wells was placed in charge. The following fall he relieved T.J. Bogy
at Fort Clagett, purchasing an interest in that post which he
retained until last year, when he sold out to G.R. Norris. He was
one of the noblest men that ever came to this country; generous
to a fault; the soul of honor, and he will be sadly missed by his
old-time friends and associates. He leaves a family of five children
who are left amply provided for.*

At no time did anyone acknowledge the fact that Jim had a
wife by the name of Maggie Wells.

For about a week, Maggie and the children were not seen.

T.C. Power then sent a message to Maggie saying he would
be in the Fort Benton office the next day and must meet with
her.

Mr. Power said, "Mrs. Wells, I'm so sorry about Jim, but my
brother and I are executors and some decisions must be made."

"Mr. Power, I plan on staying in Fort Benton with my
children."

"No, I'm afraid that won't work. Your children are half-
breeds. The Gros Ventre are being relocated to Fort Belknap.
You will go there with your youngest, James. The other four
children will return to St. Peter's. Your house here will be sold.
My brother, John, will administer to their needs."

"But my daughter Emma is too young."

"No, she's ready to start school."

Maggie already knew there was nothing she could do. The
tragedy she feared was set in motion. "I see, Mr. Power, you
are honoring Jim's wishes. How can you live with that?"

"I think I can live with that, Mrs. Wells. I'll give you a week.
We'll give you a horse, a wagon and anything you want in the
house." Power smiled at her. "It is best this way. Have the
children ready to go back to school this week. I will send them."

To answer her children's questions, Maggie told them that she would visit very soon and that she would have a new home on the reservation and that they could come and see her there. Maggie consoled her children and told each one to take care of the others. She gave Mary her silver napkin ring with the initial "M" on it along with the silver buttonhole maker, wrapped together in a small scarf.

Mr. Power, as promised, arranged for a wagon to come take the children back to St. Peter's later that week. They weren't ready when it arrived, and the children had to hurry out of the house with their arms full of toys and clothes, as much as they could carry away. Maggie grabbed all of her children in her arms and said good-bye.

The next day, a wagon came for Maggie and James. She loaded her wagon with a few pieces of furniture and a few personal items given to her by Jim. Deep in her heart, she feared she would never see her children again. Heartbroken, yet not looking back, Maggie left Fort Benton.

CHAPTER THREE

WHEN MARY ARRIVED back at the mission, she was greeted with great love by Miss Fields. She was treated differently by the Ursulines, however. Mary was no longer considered white and was viewed as a half-breed. She was to be placed with the Indian girls and was to take complete care of her little sister, Emma.

It was the intention of the U.S. government to take the "Indian" out of Indian children, and there existed no place more appropriate to do this than the mission schools. White children were sent to be educated under the tutelage of the nuns. The Indian children were schooled within the walls of the mission, but separately—literally worlds apart. St. Peter's charter was to be a Catholic Mission for Blackfoot children. This mission, as all others, received a subsidy from the U.S. government for tolerating the presence of the Indian children.

Mary was no longer a special child protected by her father's reputation but was a Gros Ventre child in a group of Indian children, all of whom were of the Blackfoot nation, which hated the Gros Ventre. Mary didn't even know the Blackfoot language.

She felt that she, Emma, and her brothers were living in no-man's-land.

The first night back, Mary and Emma's hair was cut off. According to school policy, all Indians had to have short hair and be bathed in sheep-dip, a disinfectant used on sheep. Mary was proud of her long black hair. As far as she knew, her hair had never been cut. She could recall sitting, it seemed for hours, on her mother's lap as her mother brushed and combed her hair. "You have such beautiful hair, Mary," her mother would say. "You are such a beautiful child. I love you, my child, so much".

As she sat in the chair and watched her hair fall to the dirt floor, Mary started to cry. The next thing she felt was a rough hand grabbing her chin and pulling her face up. "Pride is a sin, so stop that noise, child, or you will be given something to really cry about." The nun's voice was a shock to Mary, since she had never before been yelled at.

Emma was next. She looked so small and frightened as she was lifted into the chair. Mary wanted to grab her sister and run away, but she dared not move. Mary wanted to pick up a piece of her own and Emma's hair to save for their mother, but again, she dared not. She just stood frozen, looking into her little sister's eyes, those eyes just begging for Mary to come to her rescue. But Emma didn't cry, and Mary could sense her little sister withdrawing.

After the haircut, the girls were bathed and scrubbed with a hard bristle brush. Then they were given identical clothes and taken to their log cabin, and Mary got her first glimpse of how differently the Indian girls were treated. The beds were all very crude, with straw mats and old but clean blankets folded at the foot of the bed.

Two of the Blackfoot girls started to speak in their native language. The nun slapped both girls across the face. To Mary it sounded like a canon going off. "No Indian talk. If you do, I'll beat it out of you. You speak English only, you hear?"

The girls were fed corn mush, bread, and milk for dinner and were sent to bed.

Mary held Emma in her arms and cried herself to sleep. Mary, who needed so badly to be held by her mother, was now Emma's mother. That night she found a hole in the wall and hid the silver items her mother had given her wrapped in the scarf.

The next morning, Mother Mary Amadeus called Mary to the superintendent's office. Mary had met Mother Amadeus the year before and liked her. Mother asked Mary if she would help teach the younger girls, since she could read and write better than most of the other students. Mary had received a strong education at the Judith from both her mother and the teacher there. Mary said she would be happy to help but only if Emma would be with her all the time. That first day in class was hard on Mary. In the fall, she had been with them as a white student, but now she was treated as an Indian. The students laughed at Mary because her hair was cut short and she had to live with the Indians and wear funny clothes.

Emma was taught embroidery, which seemed to be her own special talent. Her work was beautiful, but Mary could hear the Sisters comment. "My, Emma does beautiful work; it comes so easy to those little Indians."

Mary was given a set of textbooks, the same books she'd had the year before and the same books her mother had used at the Judith. Maggie had told Mary that her father had the books sent up from St. Louis. The books were *Object Word Method, Permutation Case, Primary Charts, Catholic National Series,* and *Primer First and Second Readers in Penmanship; Slate Exercises* and *Payson, Dunton, and Scribner's in Arithmetic; and Davies*

Primary Oral Instruction. In addition, it was very important that the girls were introduced to kitchen work, mending wardrobe, and knitting and that they learned sweeping, butter-making, and dining room work. Since Mary was a second-year student, she was also taught embroidery, music, and art.

Soon Mary and Emma began to realize that their lives had changed forever. They wrote repeatedly to T.C. Power asking permission to see their mother, but they were denied. They wrote asking for clothes and were denied. They often cried together and then found new ways to cheer each other up. They were now half-breeds and nothing else.

On July 7, 1887 many people came to St. Peter's to watch the first stake being driven by Father Bandini and Mother Amadeus that marked off the foundation for the new convent, a much-wanted and greatly needed building for the Sisters.

It was a sad day for Mary, however. The Reverend Father Joseph Vincent Francis Damiani, S.J., the superior of St. Peter's Mission, was given a list by Mother Amadeus to be placed in the cornerstone, which Mary happened to see:

FIRST PUPILS AT URSULINE ACADEMY,
ST. PETER'S MISSION, MONTANA
1885
Mollie Lewis, daughter of Ed Lewis
Martha and Annie Brown, daughters of John Brown
Julie Wiegand, daughter of George Wiegand
Louse and Millie Ford, daughters of Sam Ford
Alice, Rose, and Laura Aubrey, daughters of Charles Aubrey
1886
Agnes and Babe Moran, daughters of Mr. H. Moran
Clara Davis, daughter of Clara Davis

Louisa Miller, daughter of Mrs. H. Miller
Katie Hines, daughter of John Hines
Mary Reed, daughter of Mrs. Margaret Reed (Pat Connelly)
Katie Pambrun, daughter of A. Pambrun
1887
Mamie Furman, daughter of Coby Furman
Sadie Smith, daughter of George V. Smith
Marguerite Connelly, daughter of George V. Smith
Anna Quigley, daughter of J.R. Quigley
Lily Conrad, daughter of Mrs. J.D. Conrad
Alice Burd, daughter of S.C. Burd
Miss Curran, daughter of Mrs. M. Curran
R. Ferris, daughter of Mrs. J. Hensley
INDIANS
1885 TO 1886—BOYS 15, GIRLS 14
1886 TO 1887—BOYS 25, GIRLS 35

The names of Mary and her brothers and sister weren't mentioned—the sons and daughters of Jim Wells had been reduced to numbers. Miss Fields found Mary crying behind the henhouse. She knelt down and asked Mary why she was crying.

"Miss Fields," Mary replied, "I'm not even counted as a human."

Miss Fields took Mary in her arms. "Mary," she said, "I'm colored. I was born in Tennessee, taken from my mother, and I never knew my father because he was sold to a farmer in Mississippi. I was given my freedom with the emancipation. I was lost, so I went north to Toledo, Ohio. I was given a job with the nuns who taught me how to read and write. But my name was never on their lists, either."

Mary listened carefully, especially since she had not noticed that Miss Fields was colored. Miss Fields went on. "I became a

Catholic and have worked with the nuns ever since. So, Mary, I'm free, you're free, and who cares if your name is on a list or not. Just be a good proud person. If you have a problem, always come to me."

Mary gave Miss Fields a big hug. "Thank you," she whispered.

Mary had watched Miss Fields for months. Miss Fields ran the hennery with about four hundred hens and ducks and a splendid kitchen garden with vegetables for the nuns and Indian girls. She did all the work herself.

Mary felt very sad for Miss Fields, being taken from her mother. But Mary wasn't allowed to visit her own mother, either. One day Mary saw a list of Indian girls, all of whom were Blackfoot—Kaminiki, Rose Louquette, Mary Grant, Josephine Couquette, Elizabeth Couquette, Josephine Langlois, Mona Tokomiski, and Susie Russell. It didn't list all the Indian girls, and again, neither Mary nor Emma Wells. But in large letters at the bottom was a note: "Only two can read and write."

In August of 1887, Father Lindesmith visited St. Peter's. He brought a lot of joy to all the nuns at the mission, since he had been instrumental in bringing the Ursulines to Montana. He was very interested in the work of the nuns in Montana.

Father Lindesmith was a happy man and good to all the children. He didn't seem to notice whether they were white or Indian. He had a laugh that could be heard throughout the mission. He was interested in Miss Fields' hennery and decided that he wanted to put one in each mission. Mary could hear Miss Fields telling Father Lindesmith about how one night she had to beat to death a polecat that had invaded the chicken coop and killed sixty-two hens. Miss Fields said that it took days to get rid of the smell of the polecat, which sprayed everything as she killed it. Father Lindesmith laughed at her story, and the more he laughed, the more she dramatized the killing of that polecat.

Miss Fields' room was always filled with the scent of wild sage. Miss Fields would always say that the smoke was good for her body and spirit, the exact words spoken by Mary Wells' mother. How could people from such distinct cultures, one from Tennessee and one from Montana, one Black and one Indian, be so much alike? When Miss Fields spoke, Mary Wells could always hear her mother's voice.

Miss Fields would hold Mary in her arms and say to her, "Mary, you think too much; your head is going to pop."

At this time, the Sisters living at St. Peter's included Mother Amadeus, Sister Francis, Sister Mary of the Angels, Sister Thomas, Sister Mary, Sister Martha, Sister Helena, Sister Marguerite, and Miss Wiegand, a postulant. Eighty-nine Indian boys and girls lived at the mission at this time.

Father Eberschweiler asked the Sisters to open another Ursuline school, St. Paul's Mission, for the Gros Ventre and Assiniboine on the Ft. Belknap reservation. Mary worried, since she and her brothers and sister were the only Gros Ventre at St. Peter's and because she had formed such a close friendship with Miss Fields. Mary had never had such a mixed feeling—torn, as it were, between two fears. She had wanted desperately to be near her mother, but feared she would be allowed to come only so close, and still be denied the privilege of seeing her Mother. Yet, too, she had feared venturing away from the familiarity of St. Peter's and the security of her dear Miss Fields. John Power informed St. Peter's that the Wells children would absolutely not be moved to another mission school. Again, Mary Field's remained her solace.

On September 12, 1887, Mary Wells celebrated her ninth

birthday. Miss Fields made sure she had a cake, and she gave Mary a scarf that she had knitted herself. As she placed the scarf around Mary's neck, she said, "This is from your mother and me. We are always there, giving you a hug around your neck."

Mary knew that Miss Fields was saying the part about her mother only to be kind, but she was very happy, and she loved Miss Fields all the more. Mary's parents were still very present in her mind, and she would often awaken in the night unsure where she was, thinking for an instant she was back at the Judith in her cozy bedroom with all her brothers and Emma near her. Sometimes she even forgot that her father had died, and it appeared to her as if any day she and the others would be sent back home to take up where they had left off. She preserved the image of her home life very carefully and often walked through the old house in her mind, measuring every detail to hold onto forever.

Father Frederick Eberschweiler was born in Germany and spoke with a strong accent. He first came to the Rocky Mountain mission in August 1883 and was assigned to Fort Benton with its surrounding territory. When he was in Fort Benton, he had been a friend of Mary's family and had come to see her father before he died.

Father Eberschweiler visited the mission and greeted Mary and Emma with a warm hug. Mary couldn't hold back. The first thing she asked him was whether he had seen their mother at Fort Belknap. He said he had not, but he would find her when he returned. He was the missionary for the Gros Ventre and Assiniboine Indians and had moved from Fort Benton to Fort Belknap in December 1885.

Father Eberschweiler wanted to know why the Wells children weren't being moved to St. Paul's Mission. Mother Amadeus told him that Mr. Power knew of the impending establishment of a mission at Fort Belknap and had sent word that in no way were the Wells children to be moved and in no way did he want them near their mother, since he felt she would be a bad influence and would hinder the progress of taking the Indian out of the children.

Mary was allowed to sit in as Father Eberschweiler described his experience at Fort Belknap Reservation. "If you can believe contemporary accounts, these Indians actually live on this reservation under some of the most unfavorable circumstances; they are all penned up on desolate land, two tribes who have hated each other forever—the Gros Ventre and the Assiniboine. The worst thing is that these proud people are being reduced to beggary and in some cases to a very basic form of slavery. At the present time, the two tribes number fewer than two thousand souls, which proves that something is very wrong and highlights what the white man has done to the Indians, since only fifty years earlier, the Gros Ventre alone numbered at least ten thousand."

What bothered Mary the most wasn't hearing how her people were being reduced to beggary, but it was the total lack of understanding of the Indians and their ways. Mary had a very clear memory of the first time she saw those Blackfoot Indian girls receive a beating from one of the nuns for speaking "Indian." Witnessing this was terrible for Mary who had never before seen a child hit. Mary recalled her mother telling her that the same respect must be shown to children as is given to adults. Mary's mother and her people believed in using a story of instruction to teach children. This approach exemplified their respectful attitude. They believed that it was very wrong to beat a child and, instead of striking a child who did wrong, they would tell a lesson story. Mary's mother told her that it took many stories for her brothers, and she was running out of stories. Stories were used to correct behavior by showing the results of inappropriate actions, such as disrespect for elders, wasting food, bullying, and—the worst—boasting. Striking a child only produced bad results, and breaking a child's spirit would prevent the child from growing up straight and strong. The child would always remember the beating rather than why he or she had received the beating. The story goes deep into the child and remains there. Mary's mother also told her that it is not brave for a big person to strike a small one, and many of the stories of correction told of smaller, weaker creatures outwitting those who are big and powerful.

Mary could never understand why the nuns would strike a child and then tell the child about the compassionate, forgiving God, He whom the nuns represent, the God whom the children must love.

Mary could feel her mother's fear as she listened to stories by the other Indian students about the children in their families being trooped off to boarding schools. As Mary experienced, they were deliberately intermixed with children from other tribes and were forbidden to wear traditional dress. They were put into uniforms, punished for speaking their native tongue, and were forced to observe non-Indian traditions. Mary had been put into St. Peter's by her father to enable her to be part of both worlds, but, even under the Catholic missions, she was being forced into the part of the world her mother feared: a white world where no Indian tradition existed.

CHAPTER FOUR

In THE FALL OF 1886, new classes were added to the school curriculum, and the girls were taught embroidery, music, and painting. Mary did well with embroidery but was especially good with her artwork. She produced a number of paintings that the Sisters wanted for their rooms, which made Mary feel proud.

Emma was only five years old but was also very good with her hands. She excelled in embroidery.

Mary and Emma became favorites of Sister Marguerite, who was very young herself.

The log cabin, where the Indian children slept, was always cold and drafty but was kept very clean and neat. Sister Marguerite found a way to get extra blankets for the Indian children and an extra pillow and a blanket for Mary and Emma, who had to sleep together.

Emma would follow Sister Marguerite around when she wasn't in class, and they did embroidery work together. Emma was so young, yet her work was better than any of the work the adults could do.

The summer of 1887 was the same. Mary and the other children were not allowed to go home, so when school was out those who remained would help in the garden or the kitchen or with the farm. It was also a time that Mary could see more of her brothers, who were working with the cattle and cutting hay.

One hot afternoon in September, Mary's older brother Lee Roy was badly injured. Sister Marguerite took Mary to the boys' school where Lee Roy, pale and unconscious, was spread out on a clean bed. Lee Roy had been stacking hay and was on top of the pile. He was told to slide down for lunch, and, when he did, he encountered a pitchfork that had been left against the pile with its tongs up. The pitchfork had pierced Lee's abdomen.

Mary was allowed to stay near her brother; William and Emma were also brought to Lee's bedside. The doctor arrived early that evening and spent a lot of time with Lee Roy. Sister Marguerite brought Father Eberschweiler and Brother Claessens.

"Your brother is very sick and will probably die," Father Eberschweiler told Mary. "He is in God's hands."

The children were all allowed in the room while Lee Roy was given the last rites of the Catholic Church. As Mary prayed the "Our Father," she could feel the strong hand of Sister Marguerite on her shoulder. Mary knew she was again to be a witness to death; she had seen her father die, but here was this young strong person, her brother, who was dying. The doctor, the Priest, and the nuns all kept saying over and over, "It's in God's hands." Mary could only think, "Whose God? What God? Why couldn't they bring a medicine man?" They must do something, not just stand back and keep saying over and over again, "It's in God's hands."

This would be Mary's first fight alone with death. Mary didn't know where to turn. She could hear her mother explaining to her, "Mary, the A'aninin value life highly and always pray for a very long life, but our people know when they are about to die and are ready to resign themselves, knowing that the family is there to ease their last moments. We must see to it that our people are surrounded by family. The family members must make sure that all the last proper steps are taken."

Mary kept hearing the prayer her mother had taught her:

> *O great spirit, whose voice I hear in the winds, and whose breath gives life to all the world, hear me! I am small and weak. I need your strength and wisdom.*
> *Let me walk in beauty and make my eyes ever behold the red and purple sunset.*
> *Make my hands respect the things you have made and sharpen my ears to hear your voice.*
> *Make me wise so that I may understand the things you have taught my people.*
> *Let me learn the lessons you have hidden in every leaf and rock.*
> *I seek strength, not to be greater than my brother, but to fight my greatest enemy—myself.*
> *Make me always ready to come to you with clean hands and straight eyes.*
> *So when life fades, as the fading sunset, my spirit may come to you without shame.*

Mary asked Sister Marguerite to bathe her brother, dress him in his finest clothes, and comb his hair so that he could prepare for death. She wanted to paint his face but was afraid to ask.

Miss Fields asked Mother Superior if she could bless Mary's brother. The Sisters all protested, but Miss Fields convinced them otherwise. In her flamboyant style, she told the nuns she would "destroy the mission" if they refused, since this was for Mary Wells and not for a bunch of narrow-minded nuns.

Miss Fields went up to Mary's brother's bed speaking a language no one understood. Miss Fields puffed on her pipe and blew smoke all over Lee Roy's face, up his nose, in his ears and mouth. She moved in a funny dancing motion, putting her hands all over him and still talking in that strange-sounding language. This went on for almost an hour. She finally came over to Mary and said, "His spirit is clean and free; he can go now."

At last, Mary felt at peace with her brother's untimely death. She felt that Miss Fields had been the instrument of a powerful, cleansing spirit. Lee Roy had been blessed by a very special person. Sister Marguerite was surprised at how grown-up Mary was acting during this difficult time.

Another thing Mary knew that she couldn't ask for was to have her brother wrapped in his best blanket, with his body placed on a stretcher, not in a coffin, and placed in a forked tree with his head towards the setting sun. Mary wanted to do all she could to make Lee's burial as traditional as possible. According to tradition, something from Lee's mother was to be placed in the coffin just before it was closed. Mary decided to cover Lee's head with the scarf her mother had given her. The scarf was priceless to her, but obedience to tradition was stronger than sentiment, and so Mary was willing to part with it.

Lee Roy survived for three days and died on September 3, 1887, at the age of fifteen. A mass was said with all the children attending who had not gone home for the summer. Mary had begged everyone to please let her mother know of Lee's accident and death, but Maggie did not appear at the funeral.

Mary made sure that all Lee Roy's personal things were buried with him—his pocketknife, an old pocket watch from his father, and his blanket, a gift from his mother. The nuns objected, but Sister Marguerite stood with Mary on whatever she wanted to do. Mary had been taught that it is good to cry and mourn the dead, but she would not cry because she felt she needed to be strong for Emma.

Lee Roy was buried in a little cemetery near the mission church in a coffin made by the Brothers. A little white cross with "Lee Roy Wells, Aged 15, Died September 3, 1887," marked his grave.

This was a big loss to William, as he had never before been separated from his brother. The Sisters were worried about him and tried to look out for him.

Mary was most hurt by the knowledge that her brother, Lee Roy, would never be able to do the Sun Dance, known by the Gros Ventre's as the Sacrifice Dance. She knew that the ceremony was forbidden by the white man's law, but it was still performed by all young Indians. It had been her mother's wish for her sons to perform this ritual, the Sacrifice Dance, signifying entry into manhood. Yet, even at her young age, Mary knew that under the pressure of the white man's world Lee Roy never would have been able to do it. She had to believe that her brother's injury, suffering, and death were his Sacrifice Dance. By the torture he endured, he had proved himself the possessor of the manly qualities of bravery and endurance. He had proved himself a real man and had demonstrated his tribal worth. He would be remembered as a true believer and a true Indian. His mother would be proud of her son. Surely, the Ancestral Grandfathers would be his guardians as he made his way to the next life.

It had been a while since Sister Francis and Sister Martha had left St. Peter's mission to work with the Gros Ventre at St.

Paul's mission. As soon as Mary received her first letter from them, Mary began asking Sister Marguerite to find out how they had made the trip so that she could get home to see her mother.

Their trip entailed taking a lumber wagon for a homestead in which they stayed overnight. The stage route went past a ranch on Shaw Butte. In the morning, they boarded the stage for Fort Benton. They made a stop in Great Falls in front of the Park Hotel, where the driver apparently had to tell some men to keep quiet because he feared their language would disturb the Sisters.

The next day they went as far as O'Hanlon's ranch for another night's stay. The following day, several wagon loads of Indians welcomed them and took them the rest of the way. The two Sisters finally arrived at St. Paul's on September 14. How could Mary make this trip? If she ran away, she'd merely be brought back and punished, and besides, she couldn't leave Emma. She secretly stored these details in her mind, hoping that someday she would find a way to make the trip to visit her mother.

The winters of 1887 and 1888 were very cold, and Mary wrote to Senator Power requesting warm cloth for clothes for herself and Emma. For once, he sent what she'd asked for. Mary's hair had started to get long again, and Mary promised she would never again let anyone cut it.

With the cold weather, the feed for the stock became very low. Mary told Miss Fields how her mother had helped her father and told him to use strips of poplar bark, which to the Indian pony was like eating oats. Miss Fields told a Jesuit Brother this. The Brother went out to collect bark to feed to the mission livestock. He believed that the bark saved much of the livestock from starving and thanked Mary for her help. Everyone was pleased to see spring that year.

The summers were busy, as many children began to stay at St. Peter's. The Sisters took the children on picnics and camping trips; the children loved to picnic in the canyon and to camp by the Dearborn River, which flowed from the main range of the Rocky Mountains to west of the mission. The water flowed eastward to join the Missouri, cutting a broad fertile valley on which the mission grew its food. The first serious and productive farming in Montana territory was done by the Catholic missionaries.

The Sisters were sure to always tell the children the stories of the white man clear back to Lewis and Clark. They told of how the explorers were the first white men to be in the area in 1804 and had named the river the Dearborn River. Mary tried hard to find the river's Indian name, but she couldn't. She knew the names of many others: Missouri (Big River), Maria (Bear River), Teton (Knee River), Judith (White River), Musselshell (Shell River), and the Yellowstone River (Elk River). But, as hard as she tried, she couldn't come up with the Indian name for the Dearborn. She knew that the whites had named the Dearborn River for Henry Dearborn, Secretary of War.

Mary was interested in the history of this region. She knew that west of Fort Benton the Missouri River turned sharply to the southwest and flowed through a broad, deeply cut plain that rose gradually toward the main range of the Rocky Mountains. To the west of these mountains, the waters of the Marias, Teton, Sun, and Dearborn Rivers flowed eastward to join the Missouri, cutting broad fertile valleys that the Native Americans had marked as favorite hunting grounds for many generations. The Army and Indian Administration officers realized early on that the whites would demand the fertile river valleys for their own and would need protection against the dispossessed Indians. Above the mouths of these tributary rivers, the Missouri became smaller and more easily traversed and was a favored crossing for Indians who used this area for hunting and getting to the southern part of Montana. So, for the whites, control of this area became important to the peace and safety of southern Montana. The Mullan Road also ran squarely through this section for making trips from Fort Benton to Helena.

It was in one of these fertile valleys that St. Peter's mission farm was located. Sister Marguerite would ask Mary how she knew so much about the area and its rivers. Mary would always respond, "My father was a trader and knew the area and taught me."

The community of Sisters was growing. A number of the girls who had come there as students entered the Ursuline order. Sister Caecelia had been Julia Wiegand. Others came to join them from as far away as Cleveland and Toledo. Sister Agnes had been Mary Dunn. Mary Rose Galvin became Sister Mary Rose. Mary could never see herself as a person who would enter the Ursuline order.

In Summer 1888, Mother Amadeus asked Father Eberschweiler to "bring her six girls" from the Gros Ventre country. The request was unusual, since St. Peter's was primarily for Blackfoot Indians. The mission was obviously in need of the financial subsidies which could be gotten from the government. Agessa (her full name was Mary Josephine Agessa) was one of them. She was born near Chinook, Montana, on the site of the Old Belknap agency. Her father, Bushy Head, was one of the five underchiefs of the Gros Ventre tribe on the reservation. Agessa and Mary became friends, which gave Mary a chance to ask Agessa's father whether he knew her grandfather and grandmother. Agessa's father had known Mary's grandfather, but not her grandmother.

Agessa was among the favored ones, along with Mary and Emma. Mary thought she was so beautiful, with her high forehead, profusion of straight black hair, and perfect white teeth. Why the Ursulines didn't cut her hair no one knew for sure or would dare to ask. Agessa was smart, wrote well, sang, and painted.

Agessa fell ill with pneumonia and died. She was buried near Mary's brother Lee Roy. Bushy Head and his wife were able to get to the mission before Agessa died. Mary told Bushy Head that now there were two A'aninin buried on that hill. Her friend's father took Mary's hand and smiled.

The big shock for Mary that summer was that she started to menstruate. She had no idea what was happening to her, and ran to Sister Marguerite to tell her she thought she was dying. Sister Marguerite held Mary and said, "It is God's way of making you a woman. Your body will start to change now." She showed Mary how to take care of herself.

One of the Blackfoot girls had taken it upon herself to tell Mary what she understood about sex. She said that to conceive a child one needed to have sex over a period of time, and conception could not usually occur as the result of being with a man only once. It was Indian tradition that many young girls were given in marriage before starting to menstruate. She also said that a girl should not start to menstruate until she had experienced sex. Concerned and confused, Mary confided in Sister Marguerite and asked her if this was true. Sister Marguerite assured her that it absolutely was not, and in a clear and gentle manner dispelled her concerns. "If you have any questions, always come to me, Mary."

Soon the new stone convent was finished. Mary got to know some of the workers, since Miss Fields cooked noon meals for them and Mary would help. The workers were so proud that most of the materials came from the surrounding hills. The sandstone was quarried from the hills north of the mission, but the best thing to Mary was the beautiful granite steps that came from Square Butte in the Judith basin. When finished, the convent was three stories high, with a chapel, classrooms, an art room, a conservatory, parlors, and dormitories for the girls, along with a refectory for the nuns and children. The new building, with classrooms that had slate boards and heat, was opened on January 11, 1892.

Then, in March of 1892, the mission ran out of food. Nothing remained but cornmeal. No butter, no eggs, not even a piece of coal or coal oil. And the mission was broke. Things had gotten so bad that as many as thirty boys, along with many Brothers and Priests, became ill with pneumonia. Father Eberschweiler and several other Jesuits came to help in the crisis. During this period of very little, the Indian girls survived the best. Miss Fields had a kitchen garden with vegetables for the nuns and Indian girls and could make the most food from practically nothing.

When word got out about the mission, supplies finally started to arrive, and by early summer the mission was back to normal.

By Palm Sunday 1892, the mission was back in such good shape that Father Munroe said mass, distributed palms, and left for his church in Fort Benton so that he could be there by Easter. On Easter Sunday, the children at St. Peter's celebrated mass in the new chapel. The Sisters played the organ, and all of the children sang. It was a beautiful Easter mass.

CHAPTER FIVE

IN MAY, THE MISSION hired a handsome young German man named Joseph Oswald Gump to be foreman on the mission farm. Many of the girls at the school did all they could to sneak a look or find a way to run into him. Mary watched him from the window. Joseph was a very shy man, tall and lanky, with an angular face and dark brown hair that he wore combed back and slightly long. The white girls flirted with him openly, but Mary only watched from a distance, certain that he would not be interested in talking to any of the Indian girls.

Miss Fields found out he was born in Germany on March 23, 1869, which made him just twenty-three years old. To Mary Wells he was old since she would be only fourteen on September 12. Joseph Gump had been recruited in Spokane by the Jesuits and, since he spoke German, it would be easy for him to work with the German Brothers.

Miss Fields and Joseph Gump became the best of friends from the very first day of his arrival. Joseph was amazed at how Miss Fields could manipulate the nuns in her sometimes quiet and other times loud manner. Miss Fields told Joseph, "I learned a lot as a slave—to say yes-um, Ma'am, and then do as I damn well please." She told Joseph the story of how she had been a slave for the Dunn plantation and was later given her freedom. She wasn't sure of her age, but she thought she was around thirty-five years old now.

Since Miss Fields worked hard, it had been overlooked that she had gotten rid of her dresses and had taken to wearing men's buckskin clothes. Left over from her plantation days, she had one bad habit that drove the Sisters nuts: she still smoked cigars rolled by her from special tobacco that she would send for from somewhere in Tennessee.

Joseph purchased two six-guns and two new shotguns for himself and Miss Fields, since they often travelled to buy supplies. Miss Fields was already good with the shotgun. One of the first sounds Miss Fields and Joseph brought to the mission was the sound of the guns as the two of them practiced out in the coulee (the wash on the prairie). Miss Fields found that by carrying her gun in her belt she was becoming a very fast draw.

When Mary turned fourteen, she could help teach more classes. Mary had grown into a beautiful young woman, tall, with a poised walk. She wore her long hair back in a single braid or bun.

On October 7, the teachers from Fort Shaw government school visited St. Peter's mission school to check on the classes there. They said that they were pleased with the teaching methods at St. Peter's, and they especially liked the big slate blackboards and the all-new textbooks. During the teachers' visit, Miss Fields was doing the laundry. All the old clothes that couldn't be used anymore were being thrown into a bonfire. Miss Fields didn't realize that some old cartridges had been left in the pocket of a pair of pants, and when the pants went into the fire the cartridges exploded. Everyone ran for cover, but one round hit Sister St. Gertrude near her eyes. Sister St. Gertrude was taken by wagon into Helena. Even though word came back that she would be all right, Miss Fields felt terrible. She felt like she had shot Sister St. Gertrude the same as if she'd used a gun. Sister said it was an accident and could have happened to anyone. Besides, the mission needed a little excitement.

Joseph looked at Miss Fields and started to laugh—Miss Fields got angry at Joseph for laughing at her. Joseph told Miss Fields she was becoming so fast with her gun she could shoot a nun without first drawing her gun. Miss Fields didn't see any humor in this accident.

On October 10, Mr. Madden, a great benefactor to St. Peter's Mission, was killed when he was thrown from his buggy. He was buried on October 16 after a high mass at the mission. Mary and the other children sang at his mass. It was considered a very sad loss, as he had always taken pleasure in helping to build the new buildings at the mission and had always provided much-needed food.

On October 12, the students celebrated the four hundredth anniversary of the discovery of America by Columbus. Mary helped the children put on a play, after which they all went on a picnic to Mt. Ursula, where they sang and played games. Mary couldn't help thinking, though, about how Columbus Day actually celebrated something deeply important to her very existence—the day the destruction of her culture at the hands of the white man started. As for Mr. Christopher Columbus, who had sailed from Spain with his three ships—*Santa Maria, Pinta,* and *Nina*—and had landed on San Salvador Island on October 12, 1492, saying he had discovered a new land to be called America—how can someone discover a place that is already inhabited with humans? Of course, the whites never thought of the Indians as human beings but saw them as savages and continued to treat them as such. So, although Mary felt moved to celebrate Columbus Day for her father's sake, despite knowing very little about his heritage other than that he was white, she still grieved this day for her mother's family.

Mary asked Miss Fields to explain slavery to her. Miss Fields told Mary that the first African slaves were brought to America in 1619 to work the plantations in the warmer climates of the South. Slavery became the base and structure of the plantation. It stayed in the South because antislavery sentiment rose in the North and was made a burning issue by the abolitionists. Most serious clashes in the period 1820-1860 were between the South and the North and hinged on the question of the extension of slavery to new territories. The matter did not end until Abraham Lincoln's Emancipation Proclamation in 1863 and the North's victory in the Civil War which freed all slaves.

When Mary asked Miss Fields whether she felt that Negroes and Indians would ever be free, Miss Fields answered, "No." She said that we are all equal in God's eye, but not that equal in the eyes of the whites. "Just look how different the white girls are treated from the Indian girls by nuns who say we are all equal." Mary loved Miss Fields so much and knew she could ask her anything.

A couple of days after the Columbus Day celebration, Miss Fields drove Sisters Lucia and Angela to Sun River and Fort Shaw to beg Dr. Newman to pull Sister St. Catherine's tooth. Dr. Newman refused to pull the tooth since he didn't have the right forceps. On their way back, Miss Fields along with the Sisters got lost. At the foot of Crown Butte, they found a cabin owned by a friend, Mr. Farrel, who got a good laugh at seeing this large black woman in buckskins and some nuns lost out on the prairie. The women offered special prayers for Mr. Farrel's soul if he could help them. Mr. Farrel drove them back to the mission. They were all so grateful to be home, that they again offered special prayers for him.

November 10 was an historic day at St. Peter's Mission. The new coal fire furnace had been lit, and everyone enjoyed the heat it produced. The coal had been delivered at Cascade for $5.50 a ton. But with the new coal furnace came a big problem. Joseph had sent one of the farmhands over to shovel coal. The farmhand had told Joseph that "Black Mary" (his name for Miss Fields) should shovel the coal, since the black dust wouldn't show on her. Joseph could feel his anger rise. He hit the man and immediately fired him. Joseph called a meeting of all the men at the mission, reminding them that, although a woman, Miss Fields was also a foreman and that they must all respect her or get off the mission. Joseph's anger was so strong that he finished with, "In fact, I'll personally take care of the next person who shows a lack of respect."

The next time Miss Fields saw Joseph, she gave him a big bear hug. "Joseph," she said, "you are a wonderful person but I can take care of myself, and you have trouble killing a chicken!"

On December 12 after night prayers, two Blackfoot Indian girls, Francesca Sleeping Bear and Susie Land, ran away. They wanted to return to their families. The girls were found the next day hiding in a haystack at the Morris' horse ranch and were returned to the mission. They were spanked and ordered to go without dinner for two nights, but Mary knew that Miss Fields would get food to them. She always did.

The next day, Miss Fields shot an eagle that was trying to steal her chickens. She hit the thief on its wing as it was flying. She thought she had a real trophy, but Mary informed her otherwise. Mary told Miss Fields that she must take care of the eagle, because it would be bad luck to kill it. The eagle, which would never fly again, became a pet around the mission.

Mary and Miss Fields spent hours talking about their traditions. So many of Mary's memories were fading.

Miss Fields would never miss the opportunity to mention Mary Wells to Joseph, whose response was always the same: "I'm too old for her." Miss Fields would always come back with, "On the plantation, a girl is never too young and a man never too old." Nor would Miss Fields miss an opportunity to tease Mary Wells about that "good-looking German foreman, Joseph."

One cold evening late in February of 1893, the boys came over to entertain the girls with a play for Washington's birthday. Mary was happy to see her brother. She was surprised when Joseph Gump sat next to her and asked her name, as if he didn't know it. She was teased later that night by the Sisters and the other girls. One of the white girls said to her, "I'll bet you he doesn't know you're an Indian. I'll make sure he finds out." The teasing made Mary cry but, as always, Miss Fields was there to defend her, telling the other girls to mind their own business.

About a week later, Mr. Moriarty, the photographer from Helena, arrived to take some photographs of the boys who had failed to show up for pictures on an earlier trip. As Mary served him a meal, he said to her, "Would you like to have a photograph of yourself taken? You're a beautiful young lady."

Mary blushed because Joseph Gump was listening. She told the photographer she would if she could run and find her sister to be in the picture with her. Mary and Emma had their photograph taken together while Joseph Gump watched, and Mr. Moriarty told Mary that he would bring the photograph back with the pictures he had taken of the boys.

January of 1893 had been bitter cold, with temperatures as low as 39 below at St. Peter's and 50 below in Helena. Mother Francis took ill with pneumonia and was confined to her cell (the word the Sisters used for their small rooms which held only a bed with a straw mat, a desk, a chair, and a large crucifix— which scared many of the Indian children).

Mary and many of the other Indian children also became ill with pneumonia. Dr. Newman came to see Mother Francis and the sick children. He said that they had to keep their buildings warmer, but the mission was low on coal and wood because of the cold weather, and the Sisters were afraid to use up what little they had.

By the first of February the wood pile was very low, and it was too cold to go into the mountains to cut more wood. Mother Francis gathered all the girls, both white and Indian, into one room and all the nuns into another to save what little fuel was left.

One day, Father Markham's chimney caught fire. The girls all saw the blaze and smoke coming from his cabin. When word was rushed to him about the fire, Father Markham came running over to the girls' cabin inquiring where their fire was. They had never before seen a Priest so excited. Sister Anna told him the fire was in his own house in his chimney. Father Markham ran back, but Joseph Gump and some others from the farm had already put the fire out.

On March 10, Bishop Brondel made a surprise visit to the mission with Father Cataldo, who was looking for novitiates to be missionaries in Alaska. Since the bishop was at the mission, one of the white girls, Elizabeth, took her cap and became Sister St. Elizabeth.

Joseph Gump helped the Sisters with their milking. There were now thirty-one milking cows and twenty-one feeding calves. Sister St. Scholastica, with the help of five Indian girls and Joseph Gump, did all the milking for the mission.

Mary and Emma were to spend the summer with the Powers, taking care of their child and doing housework. She and Emma did not like the Powers, but it gave them the opportunity to see and remember what it was like to live in a house in the white man's world. Mary still had a cough from her bout with pneumonia, so when she arrived the Powers took her to their doctor, who told Mary that pneumonia could do permanent damage to the lungs and it would take a long time to get rid of the painful cough.

By the end of the summer, Mary was ready to return to St. Peter's. She again asked Mr. Power for permission to visit her mother. In a strong, firm voice, he refused, saying it was impossible—with no further clarification.

One day, in Helena, Mary met Father Eberschweiler, whom she knew from St. Peter's Mission. He told her that her mother's health out at the reservation was not good. Mary communicated her concern to him that her mother hadn't been told of Lee Roy's death. Father Eberschweiler went to Mr. Power on behalf of the children, asking that they be allowed to visit their mother. Mr. Power conferred with the Priest, telling him that it took a long time to get the Indian out of the children, and he did not want them to turn into wild Indians again. Therefore, they could not have any further contact with their mother. Father Eberschweiler reiterated that he had now been transferred from St. Peter's to St. Paul's and that he could supervise any visit by the children. Mr. Power said, "Absolutely not!"

Mary, not knowing that Father Eberschweiler had beseeched Mr. Power on their behalf and feeling desperate to see her mother, went to Mr. Power as well. With anger, Mr. Power said that a visit was impossible, and that she should not pursue it again. He stated that the reservation was a rough place and that the girls would not be welcome in that world. He claimed that

Mary and Emma would be scorned because they were white. Mary tearfully remembered the wonderful time she had with her mother and father where she was neither treated as an Indian or a white—just a loved person.

The Powers did give Mary a nice sixteenth birthday party. They gave Mary a pretty yellow dress and some black patent leather shoes. They also gave Emma a new dress and a pair of pretty shoes.

CHAPTER SIX

For SOME REASON, Christmas was especially beautiful and special to Mary that year. On Christmas Eve at 11:30 p.m., Mary walked through the cold, clear moonlit night to the church. The new sanctuary lamp that had been sent by Miss Cleve from Boston was lit by Mother Superior for the first time. It sent the most beautiful flickering light throughout the little church. All the Sisters sang that night to the accompaniment on the violin by Sister Carman Dunn.

As she looked around the church, Mary caught the eye of Mr. Joseph Gump who was staring at her. Mary felt her face flush, even in that cold church. Joseph Gump was very handsome.

Mary couldn't sleep that night. She kept seeing Joseph Gump's eyes looking at her, and all through the night she felt that warm flushed feeling that had come over her in the church.

On Christmas Day, Mary went to mass again at 10 a.m. It was a long high mass. Mary hoped that Joseph Gump would be there, but he wasn't.

At noon, the children were allowed to open any presents

they had received. Emma and Mary both had packages from Mr. Power. This was to the great envy of most of the other Indian girls, who received little homemade parcels or nothing at all. This was the first time Mr. Power had remembered Mary and Emma at Christmas.

Both Emma and Mary received fine new clothes, shoes, and long scarves with matching knit hats. "Aren't these the most beautiful things?" Emma exclaimed. Mary felt that the fine gifts were no substitute for seeing or hearing from their mother.

At 4 p.m. all the boys and girls ate dinner, while the Sisters provided Christmas music. Mary could see William at the dinner table. Her brother was wearing new pants, a heavy sweater, and boots he had received from Mr. Power. William hugged Mary, who was struck by what a sad and lonesome-looking boy he had become. He missed his brother Lee Roy and didn't seem to want to make a lot of new friends. Mary had heard that Joseph Gump was keeping an eye on William at the special request of Miss Fields.

Joseph Gump was at the dinner, but the girls weren't allowed to talk to the boys or the men. Mary didn't know whether it was her imagination or not, but she felt Joseph Gump's eyes on her. Apparently it wasn't her imagination after all. Later that evening, all the girls teased her about Mr. Gump giving her the eye.

"Not true, not true," Mary said. Could such a handsome good man like *her*? She had grown to feel very unsure of herself in a man's eyes, especially in the eyes of a white man. She often thought about what a brave and independent man her father must have been to love her Indian mother despite all the obstacles.

It seemed to Mary that the winds were worse that year than most. Not only did she see the Sisters knocked flat on their backs, but one Sunday Father opened the chapel door and the wind swept right through, taking all the vestments, vases, and candlesticks right from the altar.

One of the novices, named Hildegarde, had become a good friend to Mary. Mary was heartbroken when, in January, Sister Hildegarde and Sister Rita left with Flora San Sauveur for St. Paul's Mission. In 1887, Father Eberschweiler and two Ursulines, Mother Francis and Sister Martha, had left St. Peter's Mission, and on September 13, 1887 they had opened the school at St. Paul's on the Gros Ventre Reservation at Fort Belknap with eighteen students. By 1894, the school had one hundred sixty students, and more Sisters were needed. Mary would miss her friend, Sister Hildegarde, but the one thing that cheered her about Sister Hildegarde's leaving was that she hoped that Sister Hildegarde could find her mother, Maggie Wells. Mary wanted to make sure her mother knew that Lee Roy had died and that she, Emma, and William were all right.

February 7 that same year was a sad day. At 12:30 a.m., little Lily Cash died from scrofula. They said she was so weak that she died very peacefully. Then, at 3 a.m. the very same day, Sister Veronica died. She was only twenty-two years old and had been a nun for only five months. The next day, a mass was said, and the nuns were both buried in the new graveyard on a small hill overlooking the mission. A fire was built on the ground to thaw it so that the graves could be dug. Mary saw Joseph Gump at the graveyard. Joseph had helped to dig the graves and looked sad, muddy, and cold.

On April 20, everyone at St. Peter's had a big surprise. The old-time coach, the one Mary had been brought to the mission in, had begun to run again between Great Falls and Helena. It made a surprise stop at the mission with twenty unexpected guests. Among those on the stage were Sister Joseph of

Arimathea, Mother Superior of Fort Benton Hospital, and two Sisters of Providence (Mother Superior and Sister Julian who were formerly from Fort Benton). This was the first time the mission had ever had nuns from other orders as guests.

Mary was able to help the Sisters and Miss Fields in the kitchen to prepare the food for the guests. The novices entertained the company with music, and all the children were allowed to attend.

On April 29, first communion was held for forty-two children from the mission. All the girls wore white dresses with veils and flowers studded their hair. The boys wore white shirts. The Sisters always made first communion day a special day with a picnic and games. When it was all over, the white dresses and white shirts were washed and stored for the next first communion day.

On May 26, the mission prepared for the Corpus Christ procession. The Sisters planted small trees on both sides of the carriage walk with the help of Joseph Gump. On May 27 the procession took place, and everyone said it was the most beautiful the mission had ever held. First went the cross bearer, then the girls, the women, the boys, the men, the nuns, the choir, the dais, and the Blessed Lord. The long file proceeded from the cabins past the newly planted trees. Everyone sang hymns along the way.

The final exam for the year was held on June 25 and 26 for both the whites and Indians. The students were told that they had all done well on the exams and were encouraged to have a good summer.

On June 28, Mrs. Power came to assist in the closing of the school and to pick up Mary and Emma for their summer work at her grand home in Helena. Although it seemed to be an honor, and the other Indian girls at St. Peter's were envious of Mary and Emma, Mary couldn't help thinking that they were just cheap help. Was this what her father had in mind when he entrusted Mr. Power with his estate?

William planned to leave the mission that summer to become an accountant for T.C. Power. He had always excelled in math at the mission and was now old enough to work. Mary didn't even get a chance to say good-bye to him when he left for Fort Benton, since boys and girls were not allowed to speak. She only hoped that he could make friends and that being half Indian wouldn't hold him back. William was very quiet and sensitive.

As Mary grew older, it became harder for her to spend the summer at the Power's. Here was a family with so much, a family that didn't worry about wasting things that most of the Indian children at the mission would have scrambled to have. Mary did enjoy the Power's son. Somehow, despite all that he had, he wasn't spoiled and was generous with Mary and Emma. He had adored Mary since he was a boy and often brought her bouquets of wildflowers.

Mary began to think about her future. She would be seventeen by the end of the summer and couldn't stay at the mission much longer unless she became a novice. But that was the last thing in her mind; she wanted to see more of the world, and she wanted, one day, to have a family to make up for all the years now that her own happy family had been no more than a memory.

The Powers wanted her to stay with them as domestic help, which was another thing Mary vowed she would never do. One day, however, she did ask to have a private conversation with Senator Power, who agreed and invited her into his study.

"Mary, what can I help you with?" Senator Power asked.

"Senator, Sir," she started, deciding to go straight to the point. "I would like to see my father's will and see what happened to all his money."

The senator remained very calm and looked her in the eye. "Mary, I invested your father's money in more cattle, and we lost the cattle in the cold winter of 1886."

Astutely, Mary replied, "Only the cattle you invested my father's money in died?"

"That's right. I only lost his cattle, so I have been supporting your family with my own money. Besides, my dear, you are still a half-breed and can't own land. You have been well taken care of and have nothing to complain about. Any more questions? If you wish, perhaps you can find your mother and move down to the reservation with her. Would you like that?"

Mary saw his hands start to shake and the anger rise in his voice and spread over his face. She read the guilt in this man—his offer for her to return to her Mother was a threat, extended only to end the conversation. She knew he would never allow her to join her mother, and he used her most cherished desire to drive home her helplessness. The option to return was not hers. Mary saw that it was useless to ask Senator Power about her father's affairs and never asked him again.

She was happy to return to St. Peter's at the end of August with Emma.

CHAPTER SEVEN

SEPTEMBER 12 WAS a big day. Not only was it Mary's birthday, but there was going to be a wedding at the mission. Mr. Larry was a local rancher who had given money and time to the Mission over the years. While there, he had met Clara, who was a student. Having completed her schooling, Clara had already returned to her family. They, too, were ranchers. Clara Wiegand and Mr. Larry were married in the log church that day. In the morning, Mary helped prepare the wedding breakfast for them in the convent; that afternoon, the Sisters baked a cake for Mary, and all the Indian children sang to Mary. Mary had brought a package from Helena, given to her by the Powers, to be opened on her birthday. It was a warm wool sweater. That evening Mary realized that she was the same age as Clara Wiegand, who had been married that very day.

St. Peter's now had nine houses, with seventy-four Ursulines. This was considered a big mission.

In December, Mother Superior had to go to Helena to talk to the bishop. On the way, the party crossed Blue Creek, an arm of the Yellowstone. The driver was heading for the new bridge, which just that day had been completed. Suddenly, the whole party was neck deep in the icy water. Large blocks of ice floated down the rapid current. The horses barely kept their lips out of the water. Had the horses moved a step, they would have drowned. Mother Superior roused the driver, who had fainted, and instructed him to get to the shore and ride one of the horses to a cowboy shack two miles back. However, the icy jolt made the driver unable to speak when he arrived at the shack. All he finally managed to utter was, "Nuns in the river."

The cowboys rode to the river and indeed saved the Sisters. It took several hours to get the horses out. The rescuers built a huge fire for the nuns to warm up, but icicles formed on the nuns' clothes while they waited for them to dry out. No one perished or became ill, however.

The Christmas midnight mass was beautiful, as always. The music and voices always sounded better on a cold, crisp night. Mary could see Joseph Gump out of the corner of her eye and wished she could sit with him. She smiled as Joseph Gump turned to look at her.

They all went to ten o'clock mass the next morning and were allowed to open their presents before Christmas dinner. At dinner, Mary and Emma saw William, who was visiting. William told Mary that he liked his job with T.C. Power. He had been given a room at the warehouse, so he was an accountant during the day and a watchman for the warehouse at night. Mary asked him whether he had tried to find their mother at Fort Belknap. William said, "Mr. Power told me he didn't want me to go and wouldn't give me the time off. He says if I insist on visits I could get the Christmas week off to come up to the mission."

Then William looked over Mary's shoulder and asked, "Emma, is Joseph Gump giving Mary the eye?"

"Like he always does," Emma said.

Mary blushed with pleasure.

The day after Christmas, Mary was called into the office of Mother Superior. She was scared because this was most unusual. Had she done something wrong? She knocked on the door and heard the strong voice command her to enter. Mary opened the door and curtsied with respect.

"Sit down, Mary," Mother said. "Please, relax."

Mary cleared her throat. "Yes, Mother Superior."

"You have been at the mission for a long time and must start thinking about your future," Mother Superior said.

Mary's heart fell. Though she knew she wanted to move on from the mission eventually, it hurt to hear Mother Superior urging her to go. Was she not even wanted there? But then Mother Superior continued, and what she said changed everything. In fact, it didn't sink in right away.

"Mary, Joseph Gump would like to court you. He has asked my permission, and I told him I would speak to you first."

Mary was speechless. Although she felt like shrieking with delight, she finally calmly said, "He doesn't even know me."

"That is true; that is why he wants to court you. But he already feels he would like to marry you."

Mary lost her breath. She had never expected anything like this to happen to her. "Mother, does he know I'm a half-breed?"

"You are a child of God and very special to our Sisters. You are generous, kind, and beautiful. Surely Mr. Gump can see this. You must start thinking of your future. If you will give your permission, he will start visiting you here on Sundays. It is up to you how far this will go, but you must know that if you should marry you will have to leave our mission. We have no room for married couples. You may go now, my dear."

Mary told Emma that evening what Mother Superior had said to her, and by morning most of the girls knew. They told Mary how lucky she was and how jealous they were. But Mary wasn't taking anything for granted. How would she and Joseph Gump get along? What if they had nothing to say to each other? Mary's thoughts about the coming Sunday were a combination of excitement and trepidation.

Finally, Sunday afternoon, January 13, 1895, arrived. Mary put on her new Christmas dress and walked over to the convent to meet Mr. Gump, who was waiting for her in the parlor with Sister Marguerite, their chaperone. When Mary entered the room, Joseph Gump stood and took her hand. "Mary, I'm Joseph," he said. "Please sit with me."

Sister Marguerite nodded. Mary sat next to Joseph, who told Mary about himself. Joseph had been born in Oberkreutzberg, Germany, and had come to the United States in 1861 when he was eight years old. His family had settled in Milwaukee, where his father had worked as a brew master. When he was sixteen, Joseph moved with his family to Spokane. His father died in 1879, when he was only eighteen. Joseph then took care of his mother until she married a widower, Mr. Sapper, who had two children. Joseph didn't like his stepfather, and so he moved to a wheat ranch outside of Spokane where he worked for the next four years. One summer he had traveled to Montana and had spoken with a Priest in Helena about the missions. When he returned to Spokane, he saw an ad for foreman at St. Peter's. He answered the ad and was hired; that was four years ago.

Joseph wanted to marry her. Although he loved his job at St. Peter's and didn't really want to leave, he knew that he wouldn't be able to stay at the mission if they married. But marrying Mary was more important to him. He had begun to look for work and had just been offered a job as foreman in the lead mines in Marysville, Montana.

As Joseph Gump spoke, Mary was moved by his gentle voice and eager, happy eyes. Joseph looked at her with great pleasure whenever she spoke, as if he cherished everything about her. His look stirred a memory of her own father looking at her lovingly when she was a child.

Miss Fields interrupted with a pot of tea, grinning at them. "Please, Mary, call me Joseph. Or Joe."

Mary replied, "Yes, Sir." She wanted to disappear under the sofa. She had grown accustomed a long time ago to address all white men as "Sir." "I mean, yes, Joseph."

Joseph smiled warmly at her.

Mary and Joseph agreed to meet again the following Sunday at the convent, which really was the only meeting place available in the winter. This time, in front of Sister Marguerite, Joseph took Mary's hand and kissed it when he said good-bye. Mary felt like she would faint.

When Joseph Gump left that day, Sister Marguerite said, "He sure is a good-looking man." Mary thought it was funny to hear a Sister say something like that.

"Yes, he sure is," she replied.

As she walked into the Indian girls' log cabin, she was greeted with dozens of questions. "Is he nice?" "Do you like him?" "Are you going to see him again?" And on and on.

Mary looked forward to their next Sunday meeting and to learning more about him. She was almost afraid to speak of her own life, for some reason. But it seemed that Joseph Gump was already well informed about her through Miss Fields.

Early morning on February 15, one of the white pupils, Theresa Lewis, died. She was only fifteen years old. Her family had come to be with her. It seemed as if every winter a student was lost at St. Peter's, but it never got any easier. Mary believed that they counted only the whites who died.

Mary had heard Mother Amadeus talking to the other Sisters about the boarding schools and how it seemed like they were always being hit by an epidemic of tuberculosis, trachoma, measles, pneumonia, mumps, or just plain influenza, which regularly swept through the overcrowded dormitories.

Two days later, little Theresa was brought to the chapel in a coffin built at the mission. Mother Superior, the Sisters, and all the children met the coffin at the door. Theresa's remains were followed by the girl's mother, father, and sisters. The Mass of the Angels was sung by Father Rebman, who had the most beautiful voice Mary had ever heard. The funeral service was conducted by Father Schuyler.

For this service, Mary was allowed to sit next to Joseph Gump. During the service, Mary began to think that if she died neither her father nor her mother would be there, and most likely her mother wouldn't even be told. She thought she would like to be buried at the mission when she died, and when she began to cry she realized that Joseph Gump had reached down and taken her hand. Joseph's hand was rough and strong, and Mary felt assured by his firm grip.

Mary's bad cough returned that winter, and Mary was seen by Dr. Adams from Great Falls on one of his visits to the mission. Dr. Adams told Mary that her congested chest would come and go for the rest of her life, and she must always be wary of catching pneumonia again, as the next time it could be fatal. "I must have my father's lungs," Mary told him, remembering her father's terrible coughing spells.

March 7 was the anniversary of the arrival of the first Indian pupils at the mission. One of the eleven Blackfoot girls, Rosada, was still there. Mary and Emma were still not counted because they were Gros Ventre and had been sent there by their father. There were very few Gros Ventre ever at the mission. Besides, Mary and Emma had money. But they had always been placed with the other Indian girls to live. Some of the Sisters referred to them as the "very white Indians." William actually looked more Indian than his sisters did.

On the feast day of Mother Superior, March 29, Miss Fields made refreshments for the fathers and the boys, and each received a small cake, a ball of popcorn, an orange, a hot roll, and a ball of butter. Mother Superior was given a beautiful bookcase on her feast day that the Brothers and Joseph Gump had made. The bookcase was placed in the parlor in the convent that would eventually become the library at the Ursuline convent at St. Peter's.

On Easter Sunday, a heavy snowstorm descended upon them. There was still a celebration at the mission. Mary met Joseph at three o'clock that afternoon in the parlor (now the library). Joseph seemed nervous. Many families were coming in and out that day. The novices entertained everyone with music and elocutions. It was hard for Mary and Joseph to have any privacy. Finally, Joseph took Mary by the hand and drew her over to a corner, next to the new bookcase. Taking both of her hands in his, he looked into her eyes. "Mary, will you please marry me. I love you and have loved you from the first time I saw you in the window."

Mary wanted this more than anything. She felt the veil that had surrounded her since her mother died begin to part. She replied, "Yes, Joseph, I will."

Joseph told her that he would talk to Mother Superior and would also let the mines in Marysville know he would be coming by early fall. He suggested they plan on July for their wedding. Mary agreed that July wasn't too soon. Mary was the happiest she had ever been in her life, but the only person she told was Miss Fields. Emma was such a gossip that she would just have to wait to hear the news.

In May, Dodie Sanborn, a Gros Ventre girl, came down with

an acute case of erysipelas, an infectious skin inflammation accompanied by fever. She was isolated so that the infection wouldn't spread among the others at the mission. No one knew where the infection had come from. The Sisters sent for Dr. Adams, who immediately took Dodie to Great Falls.

In May, Mother Superior gave the other Gros Ventre girls permission to travel to Great Falls to see Dodie, who was still in the hospital there. Mother Superior asked one of the men working at the mission to go with them as a guide. Usually, Joseph Gump would have been asked, but he was in Helena buying supplies. All the workmen at the mission refused to accompany the girls to Great Falls, saying they didn't wish to travel with half-breeds and Indians. Mother Superior was shocked and furious to think that Christian men at the mission held that attitude, but all the girls heard about it anyway, and it only reminded them that this attitude was everywhere out there and that they were just sheltered from it at the mission. Mary despaired, wondering if perhaps Joseph, because he had been born in Germany, somehow didn't even know she was half Indian. But of course he knew.

The girls made the trip without a mission guide. It was fun for Mary to be off on her own, singing some of the tribal songs her mother had taught her years ago, without any whites around to look down on them. They stayed a week at the convent in Great Falls while visiting Dodie, who was very happy to see her friends and appeared to be recovering.

During the latter part of May, a terrible thing happened at the mission. Joseph Gump had gone into Cascade for supplies, and Miss Fields was acting as foreman. One of the workers did not take kindly to a black women telling him what to do. Miss Fields tried to give this man orders, but the worker wouldn't pay any attention to her. Miss Fields gave the man a direct order.

The man barked back that "no white man should take orders from a nigger slave." Miss Fields very politely told the man that there weren't any slaves at the mission and to please get back to work. The fellow walked right up to Miss Fields, swung at her, and knocked her down while some of the other men started to laugh. All two hundred and more pounds of Miss Fields got to her feet and told the man to get his six-shooter and meet her out in front of the barn.

The nuns couldn't believe what was happening, nor could they stop it. The man showed up with his gun strapped on. He drew first on Miss Fields, but Mary Fields was faster, and she put two fatal shots into the man. Mary put her gun back into her belt and yelled, "Now let's all get back to work." She walked over to the barnyard and started doing her work, not looking back at the dead man. When Joseph returned, he felt that the shooting was justified and told a couple of the men to bury the worker.

Joseph told Miss Fields, "You must have been real mad."

"Yes, I was mad. That moment was a culmination of all the pressures and mistreatments of the past."

Joseph gave Miss Fields a big hug. "Mary Fields, I'm going to always keep you on my side." Joseph had to smile. He was sure that from that day on everyone would respect Miss Fields. He was right. Nobody ever hit Miss Fields again.

Within a week, the story was all over the territory. The bishop was very upset that this had happened at his mission, and he sent word to the mission that Miss Fields must go. No matter how hard everyone, including Joseph, tried to convince the bishop to let Mary stay, the bishop wouldn't back down. When word went through the mission that Miss Fields must leave, it broke Mary Wells' heart. Mary ran to Miss Fields, hoping that the story wasn't true. When she found out it was, she started to cry. The more Miss Fields held her, the harder Mary cried. Mary wanted to leave the mission with her.

Joseph felt that Miss Fields got a bad deal. Miss Fields was a real asset to the mission, and her leaving was a great loss. He felt that the bishop had made a big mistake by forcing her to leave. The Bishop told Mother Amadeus that Mary Fields must leave the Mission. In fact, he felt she had been a problem from the first day she arrived, and the shooting was a culmination of this in his mind. No matter how hard Mother Amadeus protested, he held his ground—Mary Fields must leave.

Sister Amadeus, who knew everyone in the Cascade area, was able to find Miss Fields a job with the United States Mail Service. She was to drive a mail coach around the surrounding area. One of her routes would be up the Mullan Road, that went past St. Peter's Mission. The route would be tough, as it went through some badlands occupied by many outlaws. Miss Fields got the job. The best thing about it was being able to stop at St. Peter's: She would be there for Mary and Joseph's wedding.

The day Miss Fields departed many tears fell from the nuns, who all loved her, and from all the children, especially Mary and Emma. Mary Wells could even see tears in Joseph Gump's eyes.

CHAPTER EIGHT

THAT JUNE A SNOWSTORM surprised everyone. It was a blessing that it didn't kill anything in the mission garden. On June 29, the bishop said mass and confirmed both adults and children from the mission and surrounding areas. Mary Wells was confirmed that day among twenty-six other girls from the mission. That afternoon, the bishop visited the Indian girls in their unfinished log cabin. Mary Wells came to see the bishop, who promised to build a school for the Sisters in Great Falls and said that he would find land as soon as he returned.

Independence Day that year was special. The mission had a visit from Father Prando, who showed the girls photographs of Indian life taken on the Gros Ventre reservation. Mary searched the photos for a sign of her mother but did not find her. She wondered whether, after all this time, she would even recognize her mother, and she choked back the tears.

On July 6, 1895, the banns of marriage were announced for Mary and Joseph at mass. As they walked around the mission garden that afternoon, Mary asked Joseph to promise her one thing.

"Of course. I'll promise you anything," he said.

"Will you take me to see my mother as soon as we are married?"

"Yes, of course. We'll do it this summer."

Joseph would be working in Marysville, Montana and they would move there as soon as they were married. They could make a trip to the reservation on their way to their new home.

In July of 1895, St. Peter's became a modern mission with its own telephone. On July 9, the mission received its first call from the bishop in Helena. (He was the one who gave them the phone.)

All of the students and staff were sent out into the fields to weed and kill potato bugs. The weeds and bugs had gotten ahead of those who took care of the fields. The boys and girls loved the fieldwork, as it was the only time the two groups were able to get together.

Mary and Emma were taken to Helena by the Powers so that Mary could buy a wedding dress and Emma, who was to be her sister's maid of honor, could also buy a dress. Mary and Emma were to spend a week with them. Somehow, Mary felt that Mrs. Power didn't approve of her marriage, but Mary knew this was because she only wanted to keep Mary as her worker.

In a shop in Helena, Mary found just what she wanted—a beautiful, long white wedding dress. The dress was her wedding present from the Powers. That evening, Mrs. Power called Mary to the sitting room to tell her about her duties as a wife and what she must expect once she was married. Mary didn't learn much that she hadn't already heard from the other girls at the mission, but she couldn't help but smile as Mrs. Power nervously gave her the talk that perhaps Mother Superior had told her to have with her.

It was all a "duty." "You must do things you may not like,

but it will be your duty." "You must always perform your duty." All Mary noticed were Mrs. Power's hands folding and unfolding a napkin in her lap as she explained Mary's duty as a wife. Mary understood that in telling her these things, Mrs. Power was simply doing her "duty."

On July 13 the couple's second banns of marriage were announced at church. The wedding date was set for July 23, which was fast approaching.

As the day grew closer, Mary realized that she would soon be leaving the mission, where she had spent so much of her life. She would also be leaving behind her sister and closest friend, for whom her mother had asked her to care. It was her full intent to have Emma come to live with them as soon as she completed her schooling. There would be so many changes for Mary. She would be alone with Joseph Gump all the time, and what would that be like? Though she was excited, she was also very frightened. Why, in gaining something so wonderful, would she be losing so much?

The week before the wedding, Mary had her last long talk with Joseph. She admitted how afraid she was of being alone with him, and she reminded him for the last time that she was a half-breed. Joseph held her hands and looked her in the eyes. "Whatever you are, you are perfect."

Mary said, "But you don't even know me!"

Joseph smiled. "I know you from just watching you, and I want to share my life with you."

Mary was grateful for his kindness. "I know this is right and I feel very lucky, but I'm still afraid."

Joseph nodded his head. "You probably don't realize this, but I'm afraid also. But we will get along together. It will be all right."

"Thank you, Joseph," Mary replied. "From what I have seen, I feel that you are a very gentle and understanding man."

Mary woke early on July 23, 1895. Mother Elizabeth helped her get ready. Many of the Sisters buzzed about Mary and Emma, working on their hair and helping them into their dresses. At last, Mother Elizabeth told Mary to look at herself in the mirror. Mary turned and saw a beautiful young woman, with long, black, shiny hair that her mother would have been proud of, ready to start her new life. She wished her mother could be there.

Miss Fields showed up at the mission in her buckskins, smoking a cigar. Mary Wells was so glad to see her. She grabbed Miss Fields and kept hugging her. "Thank you for coming."

Miss Fields looked at Mary. "I wouldn't miss this show for anything. I'm even going into the chapel."

"Yes, you are," said Mary, "and you'll be sitting in the front row to act as my mother."

As she entered the chapel, Mary realized that it was completely full, but she kept her eyes straight ahead. Her brother William walked her down the aisle, since her father was no longer alive and she wouldn't have T.C. Power do it. That man could never stand in for her father, and she didn't even like him. Her thoughts were absorbed by the beauty of the organ music and the angelic singing of the nuns and children.

Joseph looked so handsome to her in his new suit. Mary could feel how nervous she was and could feel Joseph's hand shaking. The wedding mass was beautiful and the strong presence of her mother was there, supporting her.

Just as they were leaving the church at the close of the ceremony, a fire broke out in the wash house. Some blankets near the chimney in the upper room were found smoldering. But the fire was put out very quickly by the Brothers, who wouldn't let Joseph help fight it in his new suit. Miss Fields just watched and wouldn't lend a hand.

At the wedding breakfast, Mary talked to her brother. William still liked his work and felt he was being well-treated by the Powers. Emma looked so grown-up in her special dress. Seeing her laughing from across the room, Mary knew it wouldn't be long before Emma was ready to marry. A photographer from Great Falls took the wedding pictures. He had been brought to the mission by the nuns as a wedding present to Mary Wells.

CHAPTER NINE

AT NOON, JOSEPH brought his wagon around, and Mary changed into her favorite blue dress. She gave her wedding dress to the Sisters so that someone else might use it. Over the past few days Mary had been packing up the few things she had, remembering to take her silver from its hiding place in the wall. Now these were placed into Joseph's wagon. Everyone was hugging Mary, and many of the Sisters cried, though Mary couldn't imagine that it would be long before she would be back for a visit. Mary gave her last big hug to all the nuns, her little sister Emma, and Miss Fields. She told them each how much she loved them. She made Miss Fields promise to come to Marysville to visit them. As they rode away, Mary felt Joseph's hand clasp hers. Mary stopped looking back.

Joseph had made reservations for a hotel in Great Falls. It was a long ride to Great Falls from St. Peter's, and though they had everything to talk about, they found talking difficult that first day. Mary realized that Joseph was a shy man and that knowing him as she knew her sister or anyone else in her family would take a long, long time. But she did make him promise once again that they would look for her mother before he started his new job.

It was early evening when they arrived in Great Falls. When they pulled up to the hotel, a man unloaded the wagon for them and drove it away. The room was beautiful. But it had only one bed! Mary washed her face and brushed out her long hair, shaking out the dust of the trail. Then she pinned her hair up again and put on some lipstick, which the nuns told her she could use that day. She changed out of her blue dress into another dress the Powers had given her. Then they went down to dinner.

At the dining room door, a fancy dressed waiter said, "Mr. and Mrs. Gump, I have your table ready." Mary realized that this was the first time she had been in a restaurant since she was a girl traveling with her parents, except with the Powers and to her that didn't count. Now she was Mrs. Gump and would be given respect. Joseph seemed nervous and wanted everything to be perfect. He ordered for them both, and after dinner there was music and dancing. When Joseph asked Mary to dance, Mary replied that she didn't know how.

"Then we'll learn together," Joseph said, with a big shy smile. Since Mary had actually danced many times with the girls at the mission, she had no trouble falling into step with Joseph. It was thrilling. Mary knew, as she whirled about in time to the music, that it was still going to take her years to stop thinking of herself as a half-breed about to be discovered by someone. To stop thinking of herself that way would take a big effort, and tonight, as her first step, she smiled and looked the white patrons directly in the eye.

Mary and Joseph returned to their room, and when they closed the door Joseph put his arms around Mary's waist and kissed her. It was really their first kiss. "Thank you," Mary said, "for this wonderful day."

Joseph said, "I feel so lucky you said you'd marry me."

Mary put on her nightgown and robe and slipped into the bed first. Then she removed her robe and dropped it onto the floor. Joseph slipped in next to her. He was unclothed, and he simply held her next to himself. Mary held him, and the strangeness of touching his bare skin changed fast into a very good feeling of warmth and closeness. Mary felt secure in Joseph's arms, she felt loved, and knew she had a good man. Joseph did not attempt to make Mary "do her duty" that first night they were together. Though Mary was prepared for it, she loved him all the more for his simply holding her, as if he, too, knew how strange it was to join this closely with someone who was still so unknown.

The next morning, Joseph started the day by saying, "Mary, I love you, and I would like to leave today for Fort Benton. From there we can go on to Fort Belknap to see if we can find your mother."

Mary, filled with love and gratitude, said, "Thank you." That morning, in the early sunlight, they made love for the first time. Joseph was very careful not to hurt Mary, and Mary was indeed not hurt. It was different than she had imagined, and when it was over, Joseph kissed her face all over and told her he loved her. Mary didn't want to get out of bed; she wanted to stay there holding her husband, but they had to start on their journey.

They were packed by nine a.m., and their wagon was brought around and loaded again. Joseph thought they could make it to Fort Benton, about forty miles, by evening. A lot of the landscape became familiar to Mary as they traveled that day. It was rolling flat land, except for the drop near the Missouri River. On the way they saw many birds and cattle but no buffalo. When they arrived at Fort Benton, they checked in at the Grand Union Hotel, which was once a beautiful hotel but now looked as though it was having trouble hanging on. By now, all of Fort Benton looked like it had seen better days. Warehouses sat empty, as did many other abandoned buildings.

Mary remembered Mr. Perkins' restaurant and asked Joseph if they could look for it. She also wanted to see William if he was back. They had walked only a block from the hotel when they saw a bright light in a window in a line of vacant buildings. Perkins' restaurant!

Mary and Joseph walked into the restaurant. Everything looked old and faded, and it looked like they didn't have too many customers anymore. But the place was still clean, and it smelled good. An old man came out from the kitchen. Mary recognized him immediately.

"Mr. Perkins?"

"Yes, I am," he replied.

"I'm Mary Wells—daughter of Jim Wells," she said.

Mr. Perkins' mouth dropped. "Oh my God," he said. He took Mary in his arms and after a moment began to cry. Mary looked up at Joseph and saw that he was filled with emotion for her. "I thought your whole family was lost. I can't believe it is you."

"Mr. Perkins, this is Joseph Gump, my husband. We were married yesterday at St. Peter's Mission."

Mr. Perkins took Joseph's hand and acted as though he would never stop shaking it. "Unbelievable! Can I get you both some coffee?"

"Yes, please!" they said in unison.

The conversation went long into the evening. Mr. Perkins' wife had died, and he had stayed on with his restaurant. Several times he had tried to contact Maggie Wells without luck, and he had also tried to contact the children through T.C. Power, who had told him that past history should be forgotten. Mary was furious to hear this and told Mr. Perkins they were on their way to Fort Belknap to try to find Maggie.

Perkins cooked steaks for them. "This was how your father liked them," he said, serving up two big pieces of meat. Mary was pleased to have her father mentioned in front of Joseph and was deeply touched to see that the old friendship still meant so much to Mr. Perkins. "You know you were baptized right here in this restaurant?" Mr. Perkins asked her.

Mary and Joseph said goodnight and promised to return for breakfast in the morning. Joseph started to pay for dinner, but Mr. Perkins refused to let him. "No way will the family of Jim Wells pay for a meal in this establishment."

This night, Mary looked forward to slipping into bed with Joseph, feeling his skin and his arms around her.

Early the next morning, Joseph took Mary out to buy some comfortable clothes, since they would be camping for a few days. He also purchased supplies and equipment; his last purchases were a rifle, a shotgun, and a pistol. This was a shock to Mary because she had never seen him with a hand-gun. He glanced at Mary shyly and said, "Yes, I do know how to use these." They took everything back to the hotel and then went over to Mr. Perkins' for breakfast.

A special table had already been set for the newlyweds. It had a pretty linen cloth and a small vase with a flower in it. Mr. Perkins had made fresh rolls, which he served with bacon and eggs and some special jam he had made from wild berries. Everything tasted delicious. Mr. Perkins was smiling from ear to ear and said he had stayed awake all night just thinking of Mary's mother and father. "Please don't slip out of touch again," he told her. "Please write me, wherever you go."

Joseph and Mary were on the trail by noon. Joseph felt that they could get some miles in by nightfall and would camp on the trail. They stopped the first night at a place called Big Sandy, where Joseph set up their camp. They had only a light meal, since they were both still full from the big breakfast. Mr. Perkins had fixed them a basket of bread, rolls, cold meal, and his special jam. All Joseph had to prepare was coffee.

It was beautiful lying out in the open looking up at the big sky. The fire was warm, and Mary felt Joseph beside her and was very happy. They were on the trail early the next morning and made it to Havre, where they found a small roadhouse to stay in. It was nice to be able to bathe, but the food was terrible, so they snuck back into their room and ate rolls and jam.

Mary found that being around Joseph was fun. Joseph enjoyed every situation he found himself in. He walked over and hit the bed, and a large cloud of dust rose up.

"Seems like they air their bedding on a regular basis, after washing it in dust," he said.

Mary said that they could use the bedding they had brought with them, but Joseph just grabbed her and jumped into the dusty bed.

Not wanting breakfast at the inn, they were on the trail early. With luck they could make Fort Belknap by that evening. Joseph was interested in the country between Harlem and Havre. "Looks like a good area to farm. We should keep it in mind," he said.

That evening, rather than find a dirty, dusty inn, they decided to camp again, which made Mary happy. They were alone again under the beautiful sky, but Mary found it hard to sleep. Her mind was filled with thoughts of what she might learn at the reservation.

They arrived at the reservation headquarters early the next morning. Mary had to give her name so that they could pull the family records.

"Yes, I was registered, as were my brothers and sisters," she told the superintendent, who leafed through the files and finally pulled out a folder.

"Your mother remarried an Indian named Bull's Head. Did you know that?"

Mary shook her head.

"She had a son and daughter by him. Did you know that?"

Again, Mary shook her head. "No, I knew nothing about her."

"Mrs. Gump, your mother died this very spring. She is buried at St. Paul's Mission."

With this, Mary sat down, and Joseph took her hand. Mary had feared for years that her mother was no longer living, but to learn she had missed her by such a short time!

Joseph began to speak to the superintendent on Mary's behalf. "Do we have permission to go through the mission and visit her grave?" he asked.

"Yes, I can arrange that," the superintendent replied.

Mary said, "Sir, what about my brother James?"

"It says here he died two years back."

"Can we find the son and daughter Maggie Wells had here at Fort Belknap?" Joseph asked.

"You can try."

Mary and Joseph left the office and climbed back into the wagon. Joseph clasped Mary close to him.

"If I had only been a year earlier," Mary cried. "Now I can only see her grave."

Joseph took her into his arms. "Mary, this is terrible. I am very sorry. I was afraid we might not hear good news."

The drive down through the reservation to St. Paul's was depressing. The Indians they passed were poor and sad looking. When they arrived at the mission, Joseph and Mary went to the convent, where Sister Seraphine and Sister Berchman, who had come from St. Peter's to run the school, greeted them. They were invited to spend the night at the mission, and Mary asked Sister Seraphine whether she knew where her mother was buried.

Sister Seraphine took Mary and Joseph over to the church and introduced them to Father Mackin. "Mr. and Mrs. Gump are both from St. Peter's Mission. Mary's mother was a Gros Ventre and died this spring, and Mary would like to see her mother's grave."

"Welcome to our mission. What was your mother's name?"

"Maggie Wells, but I've just been told she married a man named Bull's Head, since my father died."

"Yes, I do remember your mother. She didn't mix much. A very sad woman, but very religious. Came to mass every day, even when she was sick. Finally, she died of pneumonia, and we had a small service. She is buried out behind the mission. Come, I will show you."

They all walked out behind the mission to a small, unkempt graveyard. Near the far end was a grave that the grass hadn't yet grown over. Planted on the grave was a small white cross, and on the cross were these words: Maggie, A Catholic."

Mary looked at all of the others. "May I have some time alone with my mother?" she asked. The others all walked away, leaving Mary seated on the bare ground. As tears ran down her face, Mary began to speak to her mother.

"Mother, I do remember you. I'm sorry I can't tell you one more time I love you. But I know you know my feelings. I will keep our family together, I promise. Mother, I have a good man. I know you would like him. I know you had a good man, too. Oh, how I would love to be held by you one more time. It was so wrong to take us from you. You were so good to us. I'm proud I have your blood in me."

It was well over an hour before Mary returned to the convent. The Sisters had prepared dinner. Though Mary didn't mention her mother, Joseph could see the hurt in Mary's eyes and knew that they would talk later that night.

Sister Seraphine told them all about the mission and what the Sisters had done. That evening, it was evident to Mary how little concern the Sisters had for the adult members of the tribe. It became continually clearer to her that the Indians were only good for numbers—to see how many could be converted to the white man's faith, rather than recognizing them as human beings. By 1890, the mission had registered more than five hundred Indian baptisms. The bishop in Helena, His Excellency John Baptist Brondel, whom they all knew, was so impressed with the progress at the mission that he divided the area into two missionary districts. Among the Gros Ventre were many converts to the Catholic faith. With the approval of the Jesuit superior assigned to St. Paul's, one district would be set up under Father Eberschweiler. The district was primarily Gros Ventre. This meant that Father Eberschweiler would no longer live at St. Paul's. In 1891, Father Eberschweiler established his home office at Fort Benton. His district went from the Milk River area, through the Dakotas, to the Canadian border. However, no Priest wanted to work at Fort Benton because of the scandalous lives of its Catholics. Then, Father Mackin arrived in 1894 to replace Father Feusi.

The mission school enrollment was up to one hundred sixty Indian children. The Sisters were making sure the children spent all holidays and summers with their families. What had happened to Mary and her family would not happen again. Sister Seraphine said again and again that night that Mary and Emma and William should have been brought down to St. Paul's to re-establish contact with Maggie.

"I wish that had happened," Mary said, "but I'm also glad it didn't, for if you had moved me, I wouldn't have found Joseph."

Mary could see Joseph smile. Joseph took her hand and gave it a gentle, loving squeeze. Later that night, on the bed the

Sisters had made up for them on the floor, Joseph took Mary in his arms. "I'm so sorry we couldn't find your mother alive, but at least we know where she is resting."

"You were so good to bring me down here," Mary replied.

"When we leave tomorrow, I thought we could go see your father's trading post at the Judith. Father Mackin told me it is on our way back to Helena."

Mary's spirits lifted. "Joseph, I would love to see it. Thank you!"

The newlyweds were both glad the bed was on the floor so that they could make love in a convent and not worry about a squeaking bed.

In the morning, the Sisters had set up a special breakfast of bacon, eggs, and fresh rolls with fresh butter and coffee. Mary and Joseph thanked everyone there for all their hospitality, and before they left, they were given another basket of food. While Joseph talked to Father Mackin, Mary returned to the graveyard to say goodbye to her mother.

By mid-morning they were on the trail. Joseph's plan was to go south and then west and cross the Missouri at McElland Ferry. That way they should arrive at the Judith early the next morning.

Early afternoon they reached the ferry, but they had to wait for a couple of hours. At two dollars, the toll was high, but it was the only way across the Missouri. The ferry was a heavy steel cable stretched across the river and fastened securely to each bank. Along it slid large rings to which chains from the flatboat were attached. The boatman hitched the boat carrying the wagon from shore to shore by gripping the cable with a hook.

The basket the Sisters had prepared came in handy. Mary and Joseph had a picnic with cold ham on fresh rolls with apples and a pie. Joseph started a small fire and made coffee.

After crossing the river, Joseph drove the wagon a couple more hours and then decided to set up camp. It was fun to camp along the Missouri and watch that big, wide, muddy river flow past their camp.

The Sisters had given them so much food. Joseph fried some ham and potatoes for dinner, and they even had more pie for dessert. It was a beautiful private spot, and Mary enjoyed sitting by the fire in Joseph's arms.

"Just think," Mary said, "this land was my father's ranch. He had 30,000 acres and thousands of head of cattle, and my mother's side owned the rest of the land. Now her people are on reservations, and my father's land is gone."

"Mary, we must look to the future and make a good life for ourselves."

When she and Joseph made love that night, Mary couldn't help thinking of her parents out in this same area making love. Perhaps even in this same spot. Mary laid her head on Joseph's arm and was soon asleep.

Mary woke to the smell of fresh coffee. Joseph had risen early and had already bathed, shaved, and cooked breakfast.

"Joseph, you are so good to me. I should be fixing your breakfast."

"You will have lots of time for that. I just couldn't wake you, you were sleeping so soundly. I saw a couple of buffalo earlier down by the water. I thought they were all gone or in fenced areas. Maybe these two just escaped. Like your people, they don't want to be fenced in."

After breakfast, Mary helped Joseph wash the pans and cups with sand, soap, and a lot of scrubbing. Mary and Joseph were back on the trail by eight and arrived at the Judith early afternoon.

The Judith was now the center of a cattle ranch known as the P & N, Power and Norris. It was easy to see the trading post her father had built. It was the only stone building, and it stood out proudly. Mary and Joseph climbed out of the wagon and walked all around. They went inside the old stone trading post, which was now used as a storehouse. When they came out, a small Mexican man approached them. "May I help you? I'm the cook here for the ranch hands."

"I'm Mary Gump, and this is my husband, Joseph. My father and mother lived here some time ago—Jim and Maggie Wells. Would you have known them?"

"Are my old eyes seeing Mary Wells? Oh God have mercy, my life is complete. Mary I was your father's cook, and my wife was at your birth."

Mary hesitated. At first she wasn't sure—it had been so long—but now she recognized the man who had identified himself as the cook for the ranch hands.

"Pepe? I am so glad to see you!" Mary hugged him.

Mary and Joseph followed Pepe to a tiny cabin. When Pepe opened the door, they found themselves in a very clean, comfortable house. "Blue Sky, come quick," he called. The bedroom door opened, and an Indian woman came out. "What is all this noise about Pepe? Oh, I'm sorry, we have guests."

"Blue Sky, you will not believe who this is. This is Mary Wells and her husband Joseph!"

Blue Sky stared at Mary and didn't say a word, but tears came to her eyes, and she hugged and patted Mary.

"You look like both your parents at once. They are here with us now in you! Mary, this means so much to us. Please, you must have dinner with us and stay the night."

And they did.

That evening Blue Sky served a stew with a fry bread, and

Pepe made chili beans with steak. Even after Mary and Joseph had eaten their full, more food kept coming.

Mary told them about all that had befallen her since she left Fort Benton. "Could Blue Sky tell me about Bull's Head and the whereabouts of the other children?" Mary wondered. To her dismay, Blue Sky was unable to tell her anything substantial, because she herself had been denied the right to live on the reservation. Having left the Tribe before the reservation was established, she was not allowed to have affiliation with those Indians that were placed there. Blue Sky had thought that Maggie was still at the reservation and did not know that she had died. When she made her last visit there, she had heard about Maggie but was unable to make direct contact with her.

Joseph could see Mary's heart breaking all over again, as he reached out to take her hand. He hoped that he could always be there for her, and together they would have the family that she longed for.

Pepe told stories of Mary's father and mother and what a good man Jim Wells was and how he treated all people equally. Pepe said that when he worked for Mr. Wells, he had money, but now he was just a Mexican with a squaw for a wife. At least he was able to send their four children back to Mexico to be educated, and his job on the ranch paid for it.

When Jim Wells left the ranch, it had become a big business run from Fort Benton. Whereas Jim had shared the profit, that practice stopped for good when he left. Pepe said that since he was getting old, he would probably go back to Mexico within the next couple of years. Mary could remember Pepe and Blue Sky, though it seemed so long ago. The more they talked, some memories came back to her. The conversation continued late into the night. It was so good to hear about her father, her mother and their tribal traditions, and the friendship that Blue

Sky and Maggie had shared. She learned that her father had been highly respected by all those with whom he worked. Reveling in this familial feeling, Mary didn't mind losing a little sleep.

Mary and Joseph were given a small bedroom with a straw-filled mattress. Everything was clean and cheerful, and they fell asleep as soon as they laid their heads on the pillows. A straw mattress made a room smell so good.

After talking to Pepe, Joseph decided to take the old freight trail to Helena. In the morning, Joseph and Mary had a huge breakfast of steak, eggs, and Pepe's special biscuits. After sad goodbyes and receiving another basket of food, they were once again on the trail.

"Joseph, it is good for me to put part of my history together again. Many of the things I learned from Miss Fields, that were part of her native tradition, match what I have learned from Blue Sky. Knowing more about my family will make it easier to start a new life with you."

The trail they took was called the Old Carroll Road, which Mary's father, James Wells, had developed from the Judith to Helena as a way to bypass Fort Benton. It was a more direct route, that allowed supplies, brought up the Missouri River by boat, to reach the Judith one month earlier in the spring and one month later in the fall.

Pepe reminisced about the first run. In March of 1874 in Helena the ground was clear of snow and the weather had been promising. Two wagon trains—each made up of four teams of eight mules and two close-coupled wagons—stood ready to roll. The wagons were specially built with five-foot high boxes and bows covered with heavy canvas, and all were painted with diamonds.

The mule skinners roped the wagons, since they were the

only ones who knew how to work the teams. The rest of the crew was made up of a number of outriders, two cooks with their special cook wagons, extra mules and mule skinners, and a few carpenters who would build bridges across the rivers.

In hearing the story, it showed Mary how enterprising her Father had been to conceive of moving freight earlier in the year. He was really the man that had opened this trade route—not T.C. Power, whom everyone believed had done it. Mary saw a real spark in Pepe's eyes as he told these stories.

Joseph and Mary would be using some of the old bridges. The 225 mile trail had a short history, but the wagon trains were always looking for a cheaper and faster route to Helena without going through Fort Benton. Although it took the wagon trains weeks to reach Helena, it would take Mary and Joseph only a few days to get there.

That first night, Mary and Joseph camped along the Arrow River. The coulees were all wooded, and everything was in full bloom. However, the bugs were out in full force. Joseph built a big fire and put green leaves in it to make smoke, which seemed to keep the bugs away.

The area was known as the Judith Basin. The third day, Joseph and Mary could see Big Baldy Mountain off to their left. The map that Pepe had made for them was well drawn and showed all the landmarks. The fourth day, they were out of the mountains and back on flat Montana plains. They spent that night on the Smith River.

The next day, they reached Big Belt Mountain and knew that they would be in Helena the next day. At the Missouri, they took the canyon ferry, the same type of ferry that they had used near the Judith.

They found a nice hotel in Helena. Joseph wanted to spend a couple of days buying things they would need in Marysville.

The couple had all their clothes washed and bought a bed and a dining set for a kitchen, pots, pans, dishes, and basic food supplies such as flour, sugar, and beans. Joseph commented that things were always too expensive in mining towns.

Mary learned all she could about Marysville. The town was north of Helena and was a major gold mining center. In 1876, a man named Thomas Cruse had discovered his Drumlummon Mine, which he named after his native parish in Ireland. The mine had yielded 16 million dollars in gold and silver so far and was known as the greatest mine in Montana. In 1883, Cruse sold his mine to the Montana Company, Ltd., the company that had hired Joseph. Since Joseph would be a foreman, the company would provide him with a house.

For Mary, these days in Helena were almost magical. This was the first time Mary had ever been able to shop for herself, go where she wanted to go, and have tea in the hotel and be treated as a lady. Up until now, she had been the one waiting on everyone as the house servant for the Powers—"Mary, we will have tea now on the porch." "Mary, it is bedtime for the boys." "Mary, you need a new dress. I will pick it out for you." But now it was "Yes, Mrs. Gump, what can I do for you?" Mary was happy, oh, so happy. She had her own life, and though she knew it might be hard, she would be happy.

Joseph took Mary out to dinner and dancing both nights in Helena. He was a good dancer and teacher, and the couple also practiced in their room at the hotel. Dancing with Joseph was wonderful.

One afternoon, Mary even had lunch with Mrs. Power. This time, she was treated as a guest—at least for a while. Mrs. Power told Mary that she looked wonderful and said that if Joseph decided to work in Helena, Mary still had an open job offer as a domestic with her. Mary considered standing up and walking out, but since she was a very proper lady, she told Mrs. Power she would keep that in mind. Mrs. Power told Mary to keep in contact and visit when she came into town from Marysville.

Later that afternoon, Mary was still angry. "Joseph, the nerve of that woman. I would never be her 'domestic,' as she calls it."

Joseph laughed. "Mary, this is the first time I have seen you mad. You are beautiful when you are mad. Please come here."

Mary walked over to Joseph. It felt so good for him to hold her.

"I love you, and you will never be a domestic for anyone. Except maybe me."

Mary drew back and gave Joseph a dirty look, followed by a big hug and kiss.

The wagon was made ready for the trip to Marysville, and the couple left early in the morning. The first part of the trip was on flat, open land. Joseph asked Mary what her family's relationship was to the Powers.

"My father worked with T.C. Power running his trading posts. But later they became partners, and my father went to Texas to buy cattle. When he returned, he developed a big cattle ranch at the Judith, the one you saw. But my father's health wasn't good, so he sold his half to Mr. Norris. My father was a very wealthy man. He knew he was dying, so since my mother, being Indian, couldn't own land, he made Mr. Power executor. Mr. T.C. Power designated his brother John to take care of us. Well, we were told that our money had been invested in cattle, and that our cattle, and only our cattle, froze in 1887. So, we were told, it was only out of the goodness of his heart that he provided us with school and the bare essentials. Our house in Fort Benton was sold, and my mother was sent back to the reservation with my baby brother, James."

"And there were four of you?"

"Five—remember Lee Roy, who was killed by the pitchfork when he slid off a haystack at St. Peter's?"

"Yes, I do remember that terrible story. It happened before I arrived at the mission. So Mary, you have no claim to your father's wealth?"

"Joseph, how do you fight a U.S. senator?"

"It is good for you to forget all this. We will be able to start over again."

Mary knew he was right. "I do love you, Joseph."

Early afternoon they turned off the main trail and started up into the Rocky Mountains. They stopped by a small stream and had lunch and were able to watch the other wagons bringing timber and supplies to the mine.

The trail was windy and narrow, and they had to pull over to the side for the wagons coming down the hill. Mary was eager to see the town and the house they would be living in. With a heart as giving as a child, she hoped that Joseph would be as happy as she was. Early evening, they arrived in Marysville, and Joseph went to the mining office to sign in and be assigned their quarters. The manager pointed out the house that would be theirs and told Joseph that since the mine was shorthanded, he would have two days to settle in before he was to report to work.

CHAPTER TEN

JOSEPH DROVE THE WAGON up to the house, and Mary was delighted by the big front porch that looked out over the town. When they walked inside, however, they received quite a shock. The small, two-bedroom house was a mess. It looked as though it had been used by a group of miners who had lived like pigs. Mud, rotten food, garbage, and dirty wood lay scattered all across the floors. The walls were streaked with dirt. The house stank.

That night Mary and Joseph slept in the wagon and woke early to start in on the house. Joseph had anticipated this and had purchased cleaning supplies and paint in Helena. As fast as they scrubbed a room, Joseph slapped on new paint. They started with the bedrooms, then went on to the kitchen and dining room and finished with the living room. Within two days, the house was shiny and clean on the inside; the outside would have to wait.

Mary had made some curtains at the mission that fit well in the bedroom and kitchen. She had never decorated a house before, and she anticipated the fun she was going to have getting everything just the way she wanted it.

It was hard to see Joseph go off to work at the mines on the third day, but Mary was busy with the house. Several other wives of foremen dropped by in the afternoon to introduce themselves and invite Mary over for coffee. There were a lot of Irish at the mines in Marysville: O'Reilly, Sullivan, O'Neil. Mary wrote the names down with a small map marking which house they lived in.

From the porch, Mary could see two small white churches, side by side, one Catholic and one Protestant. With all the Irish living in the area, she figured that the Catholic church would fill faster, but she soon learned that there were both Northern and Southern Irish living here and that they didn't mix well.

From the very first day, Joseph learned the tradition of the miners: As soon as their shift ended they all went to the saloon for shots and ale. Joseph would have his beer and then would say, "Love to, but can't stay. I'm a newly married man and find much more pleasure at home."

The men worked six days a week, ten hours a day. When Sunday rolled around, Joseph was tired. Even so, he continued to fix up the house, and within a couple of weeks it was the prettiest house on the hill. Even the horse barn was painted white.

Mary was good at finding bargains and was able to furnish the house for very little. At the mines, families were always coming and going and would sell off things inexpensively that couldn't be taken with them when they left. Mary had also learned at the mission to work with a needle and thread.

On Saturday night, a dance was always held at the mine hall. Mary and Joseph would dance from the first dance to the last. At midnight, the mine would provide drinks and sandwiches for the crowd. Mary was beginning to love to dance, and Saturday nights were a time for everyone to meet.

Joseph was so proud of and in love with his wife. When he

looked at Mary, he would always say, "I have the most beautiful woman at the dance. See everyone looking."

As that first winter approached and the temperature started to drop, the Gumps had to keep a fire going twenty-four hours a day. Even with the fire going, Mary would come out in the morning and find her coffee water frozen. To keep warm, she wore many layers. She soon discovered that some of the other wives didn't leave their houses for weeks at a time.

Joseph and Mary were saving their money. (Joseph had begun saving his money back at the mission and had saved quite a bit.) Joseph knew that he didn't want to stay at the mines forever and insisted that he wanted to buy a little ranch of his own. "I like that land around Havre," he said. "Maybe we could raise pigs. They're easy to raise, and there's a lot of money to be made from them."

The main drawback to working in the mines was that it was very hard on the teeth. The process used to remove the gold and silver caused men to salivate, which discolored their teeth, which would then rot. All the men had to keep washing their mouths out with clear water. Eventually, many of the miners who worked in the mines a long time lost all their teeth.

The Gumps' first Christmas in Marysville was celebrated with a tree decorated with things Mary made, as well as with lots of strings of popcorn. Joseph bought Mary a new long warm winter coat, and Mary gave Joseph new gloves and a scarf she had made. Joseph and Mary were invited out for Christmas dinner, but they both just wanted to be at home alone. Mary did miss her brother and sister and had sent Emma a dress and William a scarf, but she had not yet heard from either of them.

A big New Year's Eve party took place at the hall. The women made and hung the decorations and provided the food, and a special band was brought in from Helena. Right at midnight, 1896 was brought in with shouts, firecrackers, and many toasts to the new year. New Year's Day was a well-appreciated holiday for the miners.

Mary was grateful that Joseph had only one drink or, on special occasions, maybe two. Some of the Irishmen at the mines could really drink a lot, and their wives kept up with them. Mary didn't like the spectacle of a bunch of drunken people, even at a party, and was glad that Joseph did not join in.

Mary and Joseph made love that night, and it was so cold in the morning they just stayed in bed and made love again. It was almost noon when they finally warmed up the house and got up. Mary roasted a chicken, and they had a New Year's feast together. Mary loved these days they had free from working the mine.

Mary asked Joseph if Emma could spend the next summer with them. That way, Emma wouldn't have to spend the summer in Helena at the Power's house. Joseph thought it was a good idea, since Mary had to spend so much time alone.

Joseph was a good provider and was always taking on odd jobs in addition to his job as foreman. He would paint buildings or just do general cleanup work for people, and then he would put the money away and say, "It's for our ranch."

In February, Mary wasn't feeling well and was having trouble getting over a cold. Since Mary was afraid the cold would turn into pneumonia again, Joseph decided to take her to the company doctor. It had been a very cold February, with many days staying 20 to 30 below zero. Mary bundled up for her appointment with the doctor.

Dr. Walter Cooper was considered a good doctor but was also known to spend a lot of time in the saloon. He looked Mary over, checked her chest a couple of times, and then said, "Mary, three things. You have some chest congestion. You are run down.

And you are pregnant. That is why you are not feeling well."

Mary smiled. "Are you sure I'm pregnant?"

"Yes, I'm sure, I would like to see you in a couple of weeks, and I will give you some tonic to build you up."

That night, Mary prepared a special dinner for Joseph. He walked in, cold and dirty from his hard day's work, but he smiled nevertheless. "You must be feeling better, Mary. The house smells like something good is cooking, and you look especially beautiful." He then gave her a big kiss and a hug.

"I do feel better. Wash up for dinner. It's your favorite—fried chicken with potatoes and canned beans. I also made a cake to have with your coffee."

"Gee. Mary, tell me what the doctor said."

"I will after supper, but I'm a little run down and will start taking some tonic soon."

After the dishes were cleared and Mary had given Joseph his coffee and cake, she moved over to him and took his hand. "Mary, is everything all right? You've got me worried!"

"Joseph, you are going to be a father."

Joseph instantly pulled Mary close and asked her when.

"As near as I can figure out, I'm just pregnant, so I would say the end of September."

"I can't tell you how happy I am. I'll have plenty of time to build the baby furniture. The extra room can be the baby's room!"

"Joseph, slow down. You don't have to make all the plans tonight."

"I'd like to have my mother come visit us after the baby is born. How would that be?" asked Joseph.

Joseph had spoken very little about his family. His father, whom he had been close to, had died six years earlier. Since his mother had remarried, Joseph had been home only about once a year.

"Joseph, I would love to have your mother come."

"I'll write to her and have her make plans," Joseph said.

It was a long cold winter and spring. Everyone was anxious for the snow to melt so that they could be outdoors again. By the end of April, Mary's pregnancy was beginning to show. Joseph would tell her that it was her imagination because she wanted to show. He would tease her, "Mary you are so slim. If you look hard you'll see that it appears as if you swallowed a grape."

At the end of the first part of her pregnancy, Mary began to feel much better, although she still had a slight cough which the doctor felt might never go away.

The first week in June, Emma arrived to spend the summer in Marysville. Mary and Joseph took their wagon to Helena to pick her up, which gave them a chance to shop and pick up supplies not available in the mining store.

The tears flowed with joy when Mary and Emma greeted each other. "Oh, how I missed you, Emma. You look so grown-up. You have changed so much."

"So have you, Mary. You didn't tell me about the baby!"

"I wanted it to be a surprise."

"When will it be born?"

Mary said, "We think the end of September."

"Can I stay until you have the baby? I'm done with school and will only be teaching, like you did. Please, Mary, think about it. Oh, I'm sorry, Joseph, how are you?" Emma laughed as she walked over and gave her brother-in-law a big hug. "How does it feel, Father?"

Joseph blushed and put Emma's bag in the wagon.

"Okay, ladies, if you get in, we can start for Marysville."

Mary and Emma talked for the whole trip, all about the mission and how Mother Elizabeth had taken care of Emma since Mary had left. Mary told Emma all about life in Marysville and how Emma would have her own room for the summer even though they were fixing it up for the baby.

Emma asked Joseph, "Are you going to teach me how to dance? I hear you miners dance your asses off every Saturday night all summer."

Mary looked shocked. "Emma, such language! What are they teaching you at that mission?"

Mary proceeded to tell Emma that Joseph was a great dancer and had taught her to dance, and now all the other miners wanted to dance with her. But Joseph had told them to stay away from his wife.

"And Joseph has his shotgun oiled and ready for any of the miners who come around after you," Mary told her sister.

From the first day that Emma arrived, she teased Joseph about his funny last name. "Gump. What's a Gump? That sounds so funny! Mary, you married him even with that funny last name? I would never, I say never, marry a man with a name like Gump."

Joseph would just laugh at her. "Emma, the name comes from my father, so I will always be a Gump."

"Mary, just say that name—Gump."

"Emma, I love my new name and the man I got it from, and I'm about to have a little Gump." They all laughed. Mary hugged her sister. "I hope you fall in love with a man with the same last name as mine."

"From a pretty name like Wells to Gump."

"Stop it, Emma! You sure like to tease. If you aren't good, I'll put you out with the horse."

"Okay, Mary, then I can have some miners over."

All summer, Mary and Emma kept busy with a garden and canning and making baby clothes. Finally, it was decided that

Emma would leave for the mission in the latter part of August. If she stayed for the baby, she couldn't come back at Christmas. Besides, Joseph's mother was coming for the baby's birth. Mary grew nervous every time she thought about that first visit with Joseph's mother. Would she like Joseph's mother? Would Joseph's mother like her? What would Mary call her? How long would she stay? Could she stand her stay at all?

Mary spoke to Emma about Joseph's mother's visit. Emma laughed. "Mary, all you have to do is put her back on a stage, but who could not love you?"

"As soon as we can, I'm going to bring you to stay with us. Joseph is anxious to find us a farm and get out of these mines. He is a good saver and a hard worker."

Emma said, "You know how I feel about Joseph—I don't think you could have done better—but that last name!"

The summer went by much too fast for Mary and Emma, and the two of them didn't miss a Saturday night dance. Emma was a real hit with the miners, who all fell in love with her. Mary told her, "Emma, I don't think you sat one dance out all summer."

"I will miss those dances when I'm back at the mission."

When the time came for Emma to leave, Joseph took her to Helena to catch the stage. Mary was getting too close to be taking long trips. She said good-bye to Emma, with lots of hugs and lots of tears. The Sisters reminded each other that Christmas would be there before they knew it.

After Emma returned to the mission, the house was lonesome during the day without her. But Mary cheered herself up knowing that Joseph's mother would be arriving in a couple of weeks.

Mary made all the preparations for both the baby and Joseph's mother. The questions started again in her head. "What do I call her? Caroline? Mrs. Gump? No, now she is Mrs. Sapper. Mom? I'll ask Joseph. No, I'll ask his mother. Mama, what should I call you?" Then she would laugh to herself. "You there, What's-Your-Name?"

Joseph was no help. "Mary, call her whatever you are comfortable with."

The third week in September, Joseph rode to Helena to pick up his mother. It had been a long trip for her from Spokane. Mary was very nervous, and she made sure that everything in the room was perfect and that supper was ready when they arrived. Though she wouldn't admit it to herself, somewhere in the back of her mind, Mary was afraid that Joseph's mother wouldn't approve of her and would think of her as a half-breed. But could someone like that have such a loving son? It was a torment to her that day, but finally, late that evening, Mary heard the wagon pull up to the horse barn. She rushed from the house to greet them. Joseph took Mary's hand.

"Mother, this is my wife Mary."

Caroline walked right over to Mary, took her in her arms, and said in her German accent, "Mary, I have heard so much about you. Joseph is a very lucky man. I want you to always think of me as your other mother, and I would love it if you called me Mother."

The ice broke like the Missouri in springtime. Caroline had made Mary feel at ease.

"Mary, take Mother in the house. I will put the horse away and bring in her bags."

Caroline had no sooner taken her coat off than she was helping Mary in the kitchen. Mary looked at this new person in her life. To her surprise, Caroline was very short, coming only to Mary's shoulder, and round, and she had a beautiful happy face.

"Mary," Caroline said to her new daughter-in-law, "you must take it easy. I'm here to help and not to be waited on."

"But you've just come on a long trip."

"It feels so good to move around, Mary. Now please get used to having someone help you!"

Mary loved to hear Caroline's accent.

By the time Joseph came in, the two women were talking without any embarrassment.

"Joseph, wash and sit down. The food is on the table," Caroline told her son.

After they had all sat down, Caroline asked, "May I say grace?"

"Please, Mom," Joseph and Mary said at once.

"Dear God. Thank you for bringing me here to this wonderful woman. Bless this house, food, and new life that will soon be here. Amen."

Mary took her mother-in-law's hand. "Thank you, Mother."

That night, there was lots of talk about family. It was hard for Caroline not to have Joseph around, but she also understood about the problem with his stepfather. Caroline told Joseph that his stepfather's health was poor, but he was good to her and was a good provider. Joseph and his mother both missed Joseph's father.

Mary then told Caroline about her family. She had wondered whether Joseph had already told her anything on the way back from Helena, but he had decided to let Mary tell. Mary described the trip they had taken to the reservation, only to learn that her mother had died. She said that she and Joseph had found her mother's grave and that she had learned that she had a half-brother and half-sister, who appeared to have moved somewhere near Spokane, where a number of Gros Ventre had moved, after her mother died. Now all Mary wanted was to raise her own family and take care of her brother William and sister Emma.

Caroline didn't seem to mind that Mary was part Indian. In fact, she seemed proud of it.

Mary helped Caroline settle in to her room, and everyone retired for the night.

In their room, Mary looked at Joseph. "Your mother is a good person who loves you very much. Thank you for bringing her here."

"So you think this house can hold the two of you for a few weeks?"

"Yes, I do, Joseph. I love you."

"I love you, too, Mary."

The next week was spent preparing for the baby. Caroline wouldn't let Mary do a thing, and, truthfully, Mary had gotten so big that she appreciated the help.

The midwife, Mrs. Stocker, was brought in, and Caroline conducted a full interview.

"I want a very good midwife for my daughter and new grandchild," she told her.

Mrs. Stocker had never before had her abilities questioned and was relieved that she passed the test.

Mary started labor on the morning of September 28. It was to be a long, hard labor that would last well into the next day. Joseph did not get the day off from work, but he was so worried and distracted that he barely got anything done. He stayed up all night with Mary that night, then reported for work in the morning a complete wreck. His mother told him as he left for work, "Joseph, it takes a long time with the first baby. Mary is a strong woman and will have a healthy baby."

Finally, on the evening of September 29, 1896, a daughter was born to Joseph and Mary Gump.

Joseph came to Mary's bedside to see his new daughter. "Mary, thank you. But I won't put you through this again. Are you okay?"

"Yes, I am. Look at your daughter. Isn't she perfect?"

"Mary, she is so little."

"Little, but perfect. It's funny how fast I forget the pain when I see this perfect baby."

Caroline and Mrs. Stocker praised each other for the fine job they had done delivering the baby. They felt they made a good team.

When the baby was three weeks old, Mary made arrangements for her to be baptized and named. Mary told Joseph she would like to name her after two of the Sisters at the mission: Marguerite Hildegarde.

Joseph told her that he didn't have any trouble with the Marguerite, but Hildegarde was a little much. But Mary said it would make the two Sisters very happy. Besides, it was Sister St. Hildegarde, and Mary did drop the Sister and the Saint.

Caroline was no help. All she would say was, "They are both good German names."

"Mother, look at the name that little girl must carry. Marguerite Hildegarde Gump. That is one big mouthful."

"Remember," Mary said, "it could have been Marguerite Sister Saint Hildegarde Gump."

"No, it couldn't, Mother. I would put my foot down. Besides, I do hope Mary was just kidding me," interjected Joseph.

All arrangements were made for the baptism. A visiting Jesuit, Father John Carroll, would do the ceremony. The godparents would be a miner friend and his wife, Karl and Mabel Hunter.

The service was held at 2 o'clock in the afternoon at the little white Catholic church in Marysville. Since the weather was starting to get cold, Caroline had made a special outfit with a blanket for Marguerite.

The godparents took the baby and held her head above the fountain, and the Priest started his prayers. Then he took a little water and poured it over the baby's forehead. "I baptize thee Marguerite Hildegarde Gump in the name of the Father, the Son, and the Holy Ghost."

Mary invited everyone back to their house for refreshments. At the house, the Priest toasted the baby as a welcome new Christian. Then he said, "With that name, she can only be great and do great things."

Caroline returned to Spokane at the end of October. She felt she had been away from home long enough and wanted to make the trip before the weather got too bad. It was hard for Mary to say good-bye. She had learned to love Caroline and would miss her. Mary promised to write, and they would plan a trip to Spokane.

With the baby to take care of, Mary didn't have much time to be lonesome. And in a short time, Emma would be in Marysville for a couple of weeks.

In November, they had a surprise visit from Miss Fields, who had been offered a few extra dollars to take freight to Marysville and had jumped at the chance. Mary was elated to see Miss Fields and to find out that she could spend a couple of days with them. It was a great couple of days. Mary could show off her baby and her home, and Miss Fields could tell about her job as a stagecoach driver and how she felt things were at the mission, since she had made a stop there on her stage run. Of course, the first thing Joseph asked her was whether she had shot any more men.

Mary replied, "No, they all run when they hear my name." Miss Fields' sides rolled when she laughed. "But remember,

Joseph, you are the one who taught me how to shoot."

"I know, Mary, but you became a much better shot and were faster than me. As they say, you learned too well. I would never go up against you."

Miss Fields told Joseph that she could drink in any saloon because everyone had heard her story about the shooting at the mission and everyone was afraid to throw her out. She was sure it was the big shotgun she carried wherever she went.

When it was time for Miss Fields to leave, Mary hated to see her go. She loved Miss Fields, who had treated her so well for so many years. She thought of her as a mother. Miss Fields promised to keep in contact with Mary and Joseph. She gave them her address, a saloon in Cascade. Mary and Joseph laughed. Only Miss Fields could have a saloon as a home address. Miss Fields turned many a head in Marysville—that big black woman driving that huge freight wagon in the middle of Montana.

Joseph glanced at Mary, "That is one great woman, and I'm sure glad she is our friend and not our enemy."

Corpus Christi. A most beautiful procession—the Mission was decked in flags and flowers. The day was a perfect day. The Mission never looked so beautiful. The little Indian girls who strewed flowers wearing pink dresses and white caps and little baskets strung about their necks with pink ribbons. The other Indian girls wore their blue polka dot dresses.

—The Bird Tale, Sister Genevieve McBride, O.S.U.

Mary Wells, left side, large bow in hair; Emma Wells left bottom row. c. 1884

*The Ursuline Sisters came from Helena on October 30, 1884, four of them
quickly established their school in the best convent tradition, though it must be
admitted their log cabin convent and thirty dusky little maidens required
certain unexpected adjustments. They lived in their cabins seven years.*

—Jesuits in Montana, Fr. Damiani

St. Peter's Mission
c. 1884

One of the most loved characters who lives in the memory of the Montana
Ursulines was Mary Fields. The oldtimers called her "Black Mary" and
they, too, loved and respected her.
—The Bird Tale, Sister Genevieve McBride, O.S.U.

c. 1884

J. c V. J.

St. Peters. Mission Sept. 16. 186

Dear Mamma,

I am taking the grea
test joy in writing to you.
Emma and I are well and I hope
you are the same. Dear Mamma
I need so many things because
all my clothes are too short for
me. and I will send the list of
the things Emma & I need,
We are going to have some more
new girls. Dear Mamma I wish
you come before Winter.
Did you get my letter and a little picture for Jimmie?
Please Mamma send me one
hood, one black dress, six dark
gingham aprons, six pr. woolen
stockings six handchiefs one fine

comb. For Emma, one hood three dark gingham aporns, one flannel skirts, six pr. woolen stocking six handchefs a pr. over shoes one fine comb. This is all we need so Good bye I send my kiss to you and Jimmie.

Your loving Child,
Mary Wells

Mary Wells' letter to her mother
c. 1886

St Peters Mission July 10 '86.

Mr. John Powers

Dear sir

At the request of my mother I write to ask you permission for us children to go home with her to Benton during the summer Vacation. Mother will bring us back to school in September. Please Sir let us go home with her We do not like to see her go back alone as she is sick

Very respectfully

Mary Wells

Mary Wells' letter to St. Peter's Mission seeking permission
to go home for the summer with her mother
c. **1886**

St. Peters Mission
July 9th, 1886

Dear Friend.
     please can We come
home with our Mother When
she goes back to Benton. it is
vaction now all the boys are
going. and only 8 boys stay here
please answer soon. Your Friends
                    William and Lee Wells

Dear Sir
     I do not think, would be for the better of the
children, to allow them to come to Benton
with their Mother, because she has not
much controll over them especially the boys
The consequence would be that they will fall back
to those bad habits of swearing and cursing which they
had when they first came in.
                         Yours Respectfully
                              J. Damian S.J.

William and Lee Wells' letter to St. Peter's mission seeking permission
to go home and the denial from the school
c. 1886

He was a young, handsome German hired as a foreman at St. Peter's Mission.
—The Bird Tail, Sister Genevieve McBride, O.S.U.

Joseph Gump
c. **1887**

In late December 1891, the Ursulines moved into a new three-story stone building which but proved to be a more sturdy shell for the same stark poverty.
—Jesuits in Montana, Fr. Damiani

St. Peter's Mission
c. 1893

The Sisters provided for all of Mary's wants—board, clothing, spending money, cartridges, and tobacco. She was at times troublesome, but her unfailing loyalty endeared her to the Nuns and children.
—The Bird Tail, Sister Genevieve McBride, O.S.U.

Mary Fields, also known as "Black Mary" at St. Peter's Mission
c. **1893**

Napkin Rings and Button Hole Maker owned by Mary Wells (Gump)
– Now property of Montana Historical Society Museum
Helena, Montana

Emma Wells and Mary Wells, St. Peter's Mission
c. **1894**

Joseph and Mary's Wedding
JULY 23, 1895

Marguerite
18 months old

Mary, Leo, Joseph and Marguerite
HAVRE, MONTANA, **1899**

Marguerite, Joseph, Mary, Leo
HAVRE, MONTANA, 1900

Merlin, Mary, Marguerite, Leo and Joseph
c. **1910**

Joseph Gump at pig farm, Havre, Montana

Merlin and Leo Gump
c. **1910**

Marguerite Gump
c. 1913

Joseph Gump
Spokane Fire Department
MAY 25, 1901 – MARCH 13, 1917

5—128

CENSUS of the ___Gros Ventre___ Indians of ___Fort Belknap___ Agency, _____

on ___June 30___ , 19 17, taken by ___C. W. Rastall___ , Superintendent

(Name.) (Official title.)

NUMBER.		INDIAN NAME.	ENGLISH NAME.	RELATION-SHIP.	DATE OF BIRTH.	SEX.
Last.	Present.					
255	260		Gone, Fred	Widr	1886	M
258	261		Grass, Mrs.	Wid	1860	F
259	262		(Small Face) Margeret	Dau	1904	F
		Previously left out thru error —belong on *born 10/22/1916*	Grant, Carl	Husb	1885	M
			Rosa	Wife	1892	F
			Catherine (?)	*Dau.*	*1916*	*F*
260	263		Grass, John	Husb	1860	M
261	264	*Died 4/8/18*	Crene Wolf	Wife	1895	F
262	265		Chappy Jaws	Son	1914	M
263	266		Boy	Son	1916	M
264	267		Gros Ventre, Johnny	Husb	1850	M
255	268		Caroline Matt	Wife	1851	F
267	269	*Married James Cowan*	Annie	Dau	1902	F
268	270	*# 178*	Spotted Rabit (Joe)	Son	1907	M
			Gump, Collier (White)	Husb		
269	271	Voted out by Council July 6, 1917- take off	Emma Wells	Wife	1879	F
270	272	Voted out by Council July 6, 1917- take off	Ursula	Dau	1906	F
			Gump, Joseph (white)	Husb		
271	273	Voted out by council July 6,1917 - take off	Mary Wells	Wife	1883	F
272	274	" " " " " "	Margeret	Dau	1896	F
273	275	" " " " " "	Leo	Son	1898	M
274	276	" " " " " "	Merlin	Son	1900	M

1917

CENSUS of the __Gros Ventre__ Indians of __Fort Belknap__ Agency,

on __June 30__, 19 17, taken by __C. W. Rastall__ (Name.), __Superintendent__ (Official title.)

No. Last	No. Present	INDIAN NAME.	ENGLISH NAME.	RELATION-SHIP.	DATE OF BIRTH.	SEX.
		See #147 and #148	Walker, John & Jerry			
			Welsh, J. H. (White)	Husb		
535	536		Nettie Healy	Wife	1887	F
536	537		Evelyn	Dau	1908	F
537	538		Gerald	Son	1914	M
		(See #36	Wanderer, Catherine)			
538	539		Warrior	Husb	1865	M
539	540		Taken Prisoner	Wife	1863	F
540	541		Kills All	Gr Dau	1911	F
541	542	Voted out by tribal council July 6,1917-off	Wells, Willie	Widr	1873	M
542	543	" " " "	Victor	Son	1898	M
543	544		White, Fred	Husb	1875	M
544	545		Lena Friday	Wife	1873	F
545	546		Arapaho	Adop Son	1907	M
546	547	Married to Josephine Gambler,July-1917.	White, Anthony	Husb	1873	M
547	548	Dead	Ruby Chamberlain	Wife	1889	F
549	549		Roman Nose, (Wid.of White & Yellow Cow)	Wid	1831	F
550	550		White Cow	Husb	1875	M
551	551		Lena Coleman	Wife	1870	F

4—173

Census, Fort Belknap Indian Reservation
July 1, 1917
from Fort Belknap Reservation

1880 U.S. Census. Taken from Microfilm, National Archives,
Records of the Bureau of Indian Affairs, Washington, D.C.

Marguerite and W. T. Franks
Married Thanksgiving Day, November 25, 1920
Spokane, WA

Top row: John (Jack), Marguerite, William Taylor (W.T.), James,
Joseph Gump (Grandpa Joe), Charles, William Joseph (Joe), Stephen
Bottom row: Mary Lee, Rita
Santa Cruz, California
1938

Mary Lee and Mary Wells Gump
1935

James Franks and Spike
Santa Cruz, California
1940

CHAPTER ELEVEN

JOSEPH STILL WANTED to ranch and followed every detail of what was going on in Montana. The summer of 1895 had been bad, and the summer of 1896 was even worse. Great fires had swept the range; the cattlemen who could find new grass were required to move through a smoke haze that hung over all of Montana. That year the grass, which always stayed green until fall, had started to die in July, and all but the largest streams and waterholes dried up. The water in all the creeks had become so alkaline that cattle refused to drink it. A thick coat of cinders, ashes, and alkali dust covered everything.

Joseph watched as fall game moved early away from favored shelters in the Missouri badlands. His horse's winter coat appeared early.

Though Montana seldom had severe cold or heavy snow until after Christmas, icy gale winds started in November that year. Then the snows came, and the freezing winds cut like a knife. No garment could withstand the cold wind's cutting edge. The cold wind cut the meat right off the legs of horses and cattle. Everyone was talking about the sighting of the white owls of the Arctic. According to the Indians, this was a bad sign. Everyone and everything would suffer that winter.

Joseph had stored extra hay for his horse and cut a large pile of wood for their fire.

When Joseph went to Helena to pick up Emma, he had never been so cold. All the stockmen Joseph talked to were praying for what the Indians called "the black wind," which got its name from the black clouds on the western horizon from where it came. These winds came only in spring and were called "Chinooks" by whites. All Joseph could see on this day was a cold, ice-covered frozen land.

Joseph and Emma arrived in Marysville just in time. A second big blizzard descended upon Marysville that was bad enough to close the mines for two days. People couldn't even get to the mines. They got lost just walking across the street.

Mary and Emma made and strung popcorn for the tree that Joseph had cut down in the hills near their house for Christmas. Mary was enjoying Emma, who was a big help with the baby. Emma kept teasing Mary about the baby's name.

"You sure have a problem with names," Mary told her sister.

"I do," Emma agreed, "but my babies will all have short names."

On Christmas morning, the family exchanged gifts. Joseph and Mary gave Emma a new coat, scarf, and hat. Emma had made Joseph a shirt and Mary new pillowcases with matching towels; she had also made a new blanket for the baby. Everyone helped with Christmas dinner. Joseph made eggnog with spirits that was warming to the stomach. The drink was Joseph's father's favorite recipe, and he called it "Spoon Up Eggnog." Joseph wrote the recipe down for Emma.

SPOON UP EGGNOG

4 EGGS (WHICH WERE HARD TO GET THIS TIME OF YEAR),
   SEPARATED
1/2 CUP SUGAR
1/8 TEASPOON SALT
1/2 CUP RUM OR SPIRITS
2 CUPS WHIPPED CANNED MILK

Beat egg whites until stiff. Beat egg yolks, sugar, and salt until very thick and lemon colored. Stir in spirits or rum. Fold egg yolk mixture into whipped canned milk. Fold egg whites into egg yolk/cream mixture. Chill thoroughly [which was easy]. Spoon into cups and sprinkle with nutmeg.

The eggnog was a holiday treat. Mary had only one eggnog, as she was afraid the spirits would get into her milk.

Mary enjoyed that Christmas. It was a real family Christmas for her, and she was truly happy.

On January 9, 1897, it snowed without stopping for sixteen hours, as much as an inch an hour. The temperature fell to 22 below zero, delaying Emma's leaving. Snow continued to fall on and off for another ten days, with temperatures ranging from 22 below to 46 below.

A small break in the weather came, and Emma was able to get a ride to Helena on a wagon going for supplies. It was a blessing that she was able to leave at that time, because on January 28, the great blizzard struck. It stormed for three days and nights, and again the mines were closed. People couldn't see ten feet in front of them. The thermometer plummeted to 65 below zero. At last, a sudden break from the cold and wind came, and everyone started shouting "Chinook!" But the break didn't last, and another storm set in and lasted until February. Snow was waist deep, and the drifts were higher than the houses.

Reports came in about what happened to a herd of cattle during this long cold spell. The herd had been driven across the Missouri in early fall to feed on better grass on the northern range. Because little shelter existed on the steppes north of the river, the cattle were half dead from cold and hunger. Bewildered and blinded from the snow, they had blundered into barbed-wire fences and crumpled against them. Many perished. They were trapped in drifts up to their bellies and stood erect until they froze. Some had fallen into air holes in the river.

It was impossible to tell how cold it was. A newspaper report described how cowboys dealt with the cold. The cowboys had to don two suits of heavy underwear, two pairs of wool socks, wool pants, two woolen shirts, overalls, leather chaps, wool gloves under leather mittens, heavy blanket-lined overcoats and fur caps pulled over their ears. Before putting on their socks, they would walk in the snow in their bare feet. The chill would cause the feet to warm up. Then they would rub their feet dry, pull on their riding boots, stand in water, go outside until an airtight sheath of ice would form on their boots. Some wore fur moccasins and overshoes or sheepskin boots.

The cowboys worked to extricate cattle caught in the drifts and tried to herd the dying cattle into ravines for shelter. They also tried to push them away from the treacherous river.

The smart cowboys blackened their faces and eyes with lampblack or burnt matches to stop snow blindness. They wrapped wool cloth around their faces and cut eyeholes. They would tie themselves in their saddle, but the icy air cut into their lungs and stomachs; their hands and feet froze. Many of them died and were found tied and frozen to their horses. As Mary and Joseph read the reports, they were grateful to still be at the mines in their warm house.

At the most, the cowboys made forty dollars a month. Joseph was making more than twice that, and he had a house thrown in besides. But he still wanted a ranch. He wasn't going to raise cattle or sheep but had decided on hogs. There was a great demand for pork, and hogs could be kept in sheds. Joseph had never heard of a pig freezing.

The storm continued through February. The tragedy of the range was brought into the towns. Starving cattle wandered into every town and collapsed and died in doorways. Five thousand head of cattle poured into Great Falls and couldn't be driven out.

Mary was happy to have the baby for company, since it was almost impossible for her to get out to visit friends, and with Joseph at the mines, the days were long.

Montana always had a chinook in February, but this year it didn't come until March. It had been a long, cold, hard winter.

Joseph felt that spring might be a good time to buy a ranch. He figured that many would want out of the cattle and sheep business. He was interested to see what the losses would be from this blizzard. The cattlemen would know by May and were feeling lucky. If the winter had lasted twenty more days, it would have been a total loss for everyone.

In early May, the reports from the ranchers started to come in. The news was sad. Just a short ride from their houses, the ranchers could see thousands of rotting cattle carcasses everywhere on the plains. Where the cattle had taken refuge in the coulees and valleys, the cattlemen could not enter because of the stench of decomposing cattle.

The estimates kept coming in. After the roundups had been completed, there was a report of a 60 percent loss for the state of Montana, or more than 365,000 head. The loss amounted to twenty million dollars. The cattlemen had to figure in the deterioration of their potential assets, including unborn calves, the cost of restocking, the time to build a new herd, and the cost of keeping a crew on the range. Some cattlemen tried to sell the hides from the dead cattle, but they received only a little more than a dollar a hide. One after another, the big cattle companies went bankrupt.

Joseph quit his job in June, and he and Mary loaded their belongings into the wagon. Joseph had told Mary that it was time for them to start their own small ranch. As Mary packed up their things, she knew she would always fondly remember this first house of theirs. Before they left, several of the other miners and their wives threw a party for them. Everyone was sad to see little Marguerite go.

The mine told Joseph he could have his job back anytime he wanted to return to Marysville.

Joseph seemed to know right where he wanted to go. He and Mary rode north, through Great Falls, stopping for the night at the mission. This gave Joseph a chance to see his old friends and Mary to see Emma and the Sisters at the mission. Best of all, they could show everyone their baby.

The first to greet them was Miss Fields, who was also visiting. You could hear her half a mile away. "Mary, Joseph, let me see that baby again." "Been a long time." "She sure grown. Oh, how wonderful." "Come into the kitchen." "Still my kitchen." "No one big enough round here to throw me out when I visit." "Coffee, cake, please sit!"

As Mary gave Miss Fields a big hug, Miss Fields said, "It is so good to see you here at the mission. Have you seen Emma yet?"

"Emma is in her class but will be out soon."

Joseph said, "I'm going to put up the horse and get us a room for the night. See you later."

"I will be right here," Mary said. "I do want to find Emma."

The mission hadn't changed since Mary had left. The Sisters

brought Mary up on all the news of the mission. One of the Brothers told Joseph a funny story. In February, a crazy man was running around the mission shooting at random. "Scared the hell out of the nuns—bullets whizzing by them. When they were coming from Benediction, they all hid in the snow. Father went out to grab the man, but he couldn't find him. Joseph, you should have seen those nuns. Like a covey of quail going all directions. Those were some unhappy nuns."

Joseph couldn't stop laughing as he remembered seeing the nuns falling on the ice on the way to church. It was easy to picture them diving into the snow as the bullets whizzed past.

Mary remembered that Miss Fields had a birthday on March 15. "Which one was this?" Mary asked.

"I was 64 years old. Was born in 1832. Sure seems a long time ago."

"Mary," one of the nuns broke in, "you just missed the feast of Corpus Christi. Emma helped. We had the most beautiful procession. The children made flags and picked flowers. They decorated the whole mission. It was the first big day after the long winter. The little Indian girls strewed flowers during the procession. They were all wearing their pink dresses and white caps, with baskets strung around their necks on pink ribbons. The older Indian girls wore their blue polka dot dresses."

Mary always liked Miss Fields, and she was very pleased that Miss Fields was there. Miss Fields enjoyed everything, including her work.

"Ah, Mary, here comes Emma!" One of the nuns pointed to Emma coming from the classroom building. Emma came bounding into the kitchen, and she and Mary hugged.

"Let me see the baby. You know she is my only niece. She is beautiful! Look at those big black eyes and all that hair. I made her a new bonnet."

Emma and Mary had some time to talk before dinner. Mary told her sister about their plans to buy a ranch. As soon as she and Joseph were settled, they would send for her to live with them if she wanted.

At dinner that night, Mary was able to see all the nuns and had an opportunity to thank Mother Elizabeth for watching out for Emma. Baby Marguerite was the highlight of the evening. She was so good as she was passed from one person to the next.

Mary and Joseph stayed in the guest room near the Priests' quarters. It was a nice room, kept for special guests, including the bishop. Mary and Joseph stayed two days, and everyone wanted them to stay longer, but Joseph wanted to be back on the trail again.

Mary was enjoying the trip and liked camping along the trail. Joseph seemed to know right where he wanted to go. When he reached the top to where he could go either east to Harlem and the Fort Belknap Reservation or west, he turned toward the west. It was amazing how much land was for sale. Within a couple of days, Joseph had located a small ranch on the Milk River. The owner, Mr. Hastings, had one hundred forty acres and a house with a large barn. The land was all fenced and had good water and was situated along the Milk River. Mr. Hastings had lost ninety percent of his cattle and was living on borrowed money. He was asking two thousand dollars for the whole place. Joseph offered him fifteen hundred dollars cash with a promise to take over as soon as he could. The two men struck a deal. Joseph and Mary would camp on the land, and Joseph could start building hog pens and looking for pregnant sows. He would also need to find a good boar for breeding.

Mary was able to help Mabel Hastings with her packing. It was hard for Mrs. Hasting to leave her home, but the Hastings were going to move back east. In some ways, they were happy to be leaving Montana.

The house was beautiful. It had a big kitchen, living room, and four bedrooms. The Hastings had hoped to have a family but hadn't been blessed with children.

The changes took only a week. Joseph bought Hastings' few remaining head of cattle as well as his hay cutter and a team of good horses for plowing. Joseph was satisfied that he had made a good deal. He had gotten set up and equipped for under two thousand dollars. The Hastings were pleased, too, since very few people had been able to sell their farms and were just packing up and leaving.

It was easy for Joseph to buy sows from the farmers who were leaving, and before long he had twenty-five, all ready to have litters. This kept Joseph busy building small houses and a separate shed for each sow. Joseph also planted corn and started cutting hay for the following winter. In his spare time, he started a smokehouse. He had learned a lot at the mission, and he was planning to cure the best ham and bacon in the whole territory.

Before long, Mary had the whole house decorated. She just loved having a home of her own. Emma would be joining them by the end of August to live with them for good. Joseph would often look at Mary and say, "How am I going to live in a house with three women?"

"Joseph, you can always move out with the pigs."

"Thanks, Mary."

When Emma finally arrived, Mary was so happy to have her there, since between canning for winter and drying corn and taking care of the baby, she was very busy. Emma was so happy to have a room to herself for the first time in her life.

Everyone kept busy preparing for winter. The sows all had litters, and with an average of ten little piggies, as Mary would call them, per litter, Joseph had to prepare for winter for over two hundred fifty pigs. He was happy with his stock and would have almost double that amount by next spring.

"Joseph, how do you explain that you are a 'pig rancher' in Montana?" asked Emma.

"If we make money, who cares what they call me?"

The house was well built and easy to warm. In fact, the wood cook stove produced almost enough heat if room doors were left open.

September 12 was Mary's nineteenth birthday, and Emma made Mary a cake and also made her a new dress.

"Emma, you sew so beautifully. I only wish I had some of your talent."

"Yes, but your paintings were much better than mine. Look at that beautiful one you did of the mission over on the wall."

"I am proud of that one," Mary confessed.

Joseph gave Mary a new Canadian blanket coat, a big red plaid thing.

"Thank you, everyone, for this birthday. I only wish William could be here. But he did say he would come for Christmas."

September 29 was Marguerite's first birthday. The toddler was walking and getting into everything. Joseph had to build a fence around the stove and fireplace to keep her safe. Emma made her clothes, and Joseph made her a rocking chair.

It turned cold early again that year, but no big snows fell before Christmas. It was another wonderful Christmas for Mary, with Joseph, Marguerite, Emma, and William to celebrate with her. Emma and Mary cooked and baked for days before Christmas.

William arrived two days before Christmas and stayed until after New Year's. Joseph went into the hills to get a tree, and everyone helped to decorate it with candles and strings of berries and popcorn. Mary and Emma made cloth angels and hung cookies. The tree was beautiful.

On Christmas, the family exchanged gifts. Joseph had made blocks and a small table and chair for Marguerite. He had also bought her a beautiful porcelain doll.

"Joseph, where did you get that beautiful doll?"

"I got it in Helena and kept it hidden!"

"Well, I've got something hidden, too."

"What?" Joseph's eyes widened.

At dinner that night, Mary announced that she was pregnant and would be having another baby in July.

"I hope it's a boy. I'll need some defense with all these women around," Joseph exclaimed.

"This will be good. I will be with you this time," Emma said, hugging her sister.

"Emma, with two around, I will really need you."

William told of his work at Fort Benton with Power's company. He was the company's accountant and still enjoyed the work. He had a girlfriend named Flora, who was white. Apparently a lot of people were not too happy that she was going out with a "half-breed." But nothing seemed to bother her, and she was proud to be seen with William.

"Are we going to have a wedding? Joseph asked. "If so, give me a little time so I can get someone to watch this place."

"Joseph," William responded, "if a wedding is planned I will give you plenty of notice."

It had been a good Christmas. Mary was so happy to have her family around. They had a New Year's party with only the family. When midnight arrived, they all stood out on the porch and banged on pots with wooden spoons. The farm was so far from their neighbors that only the pigs, the horses, and the cows could hear all their noise.

Mary watched her happy family as they gaily banged on the pots. "Please," she pleaded, "don't break my wooden spoons. They are very hard to find."

"Happy New Year," Joseph said as he hugged Mary. "It is now 1898, and if they break your spoons, I will make you new ones."

Two days later, William returned to Fort Benton. It was good that he left when he did, because right after he left a big storm hit. The temperature was so cold and the wind was blowing so hard that Joseph had to tie a rope from the house to the barn so that he wouldn't get lost when he went out to feed his stock. The only thing they could hope for was that it would not be a long snow and the Chinooks would come early.

Mary and Emma spent the cold periods sewing, cooking, and taking care of Marguerite.

Mary always kept a pot of hot coffee on the stove. Joseph liked his hot coffee, especially after being out in thirty below weather feeding the livestock. In the morning, he would put a little whiskey in a cup. Then he would wink at Mary and Emma as he explained, "Gets my blood moving."

"You mean, Joseph, to keep you warm out in that barn."

The barn was warm with all that livestock, and Joseph had put feedsacks over large openings so that the pigs could go out into their pens and push around in the snow, then come back in.

When the chinook was approaching, the temperature would slowly start to rise. Big black clouds would appear on the western horizon and bring warm winds, which caused the snow to melt. This didn't mean the end of storms, but it usually meant that the bad ones were over. As soon as the snow melted, the new grass would start to grow.

When the weather started to break, Joseph hired two men to help him slaughter the pigs from the previous year. The pigs were cut up and put in the smokehouse. Joseph asked Mary whether she and Emma would be interested in making sausages. They said they would try it. Joseph had learned from the German Brothers at the mission how to prepare pork and not waste a thing.

It was a busy spring. As soon as Joseph had a wagonload of smoked pork, he hired a man to stay at the ranch and headed for Fort Benton and Great Falls. His smoked pork was a hit with the army, with hotels, and with butchers. Joseph was able to sell his load of pork and had orders for as much as he could produce. The only stipulation he made was that anyone who wanted more had to pick it up at the ranch. When Joseph returned to the ranch, he built a small butcher shop near the trail. He hand-painted a sign that said, "Joseph's Best Smoked Pork in Montana."

Joseph also found that many of the ranchers were willing to buy hay. He figured that they were able to cut only one crop of hay a year, but he discovered that if he diverted the Milk River, he could cut two crops by flooding his fields. Joseph had hired a new hand, Charlie Randall, who was working out well. Charlie had set up his quarters in the upper part of the barn but ate all meals at the house. Joseph paid him forty-five dollars a month plus food.

One of the big cattle ranchers was Herman Holland, a tough little German, who wanted to buy all the hay Joseph could produce. Joseph liked Mr. Holland. They were able to speak German together, and Joseph felt that Mr. Holland was a hard worker, even though he didn't know anything about ranching. It wasn't long before Herman Holland had offered Joseph a job to help him do the planning, the branding, even the castrating on his ranch, as well as to figure how much hay was needed per cattle head. Mr. Holland offered to pay Joseph one hundred dollars for his help.

Joseph was one busy man, but he was making a good living

and could afford to start buying more land. The cattlemen were curious. They hated the sheepmen, but a pigman was something different. Mr. Holland's men all respected Joseph, who really knew his livestock.

Joseph didn't have much time to spend with his family, since this was one of his busiest springs. Mary was getting closer to her due date. Joseph had asked Mrs. Holland who had lots of experience as a midwife, whether she could help with the birth of their second child.

Mary and Joseph's second child, a son, was born on July 14, 1898, at six in the evening. Mary wanted to name the baby after the Power's son, Merlin. Joseph wasn't too sure about this, since Senator Power hadn't done much for Mary's family. Mary said, "I have taken care of this boy, and I do love him. And I love the name Merlin." Joseph persuaded Mary to use the name for their next son, and they agreed on Leo for their first son. Joseph liked the name—at least it wasn't as long as Marguerite Hildegarde.

The village of Havre had a small Catholic church, and Mary knew the Priest, Father Foller. Mary arranged for the baby's baptism in August.

It was hard for the cattlemen to recover from the difficult winter, yet the sheep ranchers were starting to hold their own. In 1885, the number of sheep and cattle in Montana were nearly equal: 593,896 sheep and 509,768 cattle. While the cattle industry was teetering on the brink of ruin, the sheep industry was expanding. By 1886, there were 968,298 sheep, and by 1898, there were more than one and one-half million.

Even with their hatred of sheep, many cattlemen were turning to sheep. Joseph had a few and Mr. Holland was bringing in a thousand head. In 1898, since it cost about twenty dollars a head to get started in the cattle business, it would take about twenty thousand dollars to put one thousand head of cattle on the range. However, since the value of sheep was only two dollars and thirty-five cents a head, the cost of starting in the sheep business with the same thousand head was only twenty-three hundred fifty dollars. Though the return per head on sheep was much lower, sheep multiplied much quicker. The sheep breeders would calculate a net profit of from twenty-five percent to thirty percent. Lambs became producers the first year, while calves were unproductive for several years. Also, sheep produced two profits: one from mutton and one from wool. Wool was cut twice a year, while cattle produced a hide only when they were slaughtered.

This year, the sheep would produce 7.78 million pounds of wool. The average price of wool was about twenty-five cents a pound. Crews of men traveled from ranch to ranch who did nothing but sheer sheep. Billings, Montana, became the center for shipping both sheep and wool to the East.

Montana was growing, and not all its profit was in cattle and sheep. Montana was making money in its mines and in timber. The gold and silver mines were producing millions of dollars per year, and now copper was out-producing both gold and silver. In 1888 over seven million dollars in copper and a half a million dollars in lead were produced in Montana.

Anaconda was using forty thousand feet of timber a day in the mines and was contracting for over one million in lumber a year.

The big news was the jump in population. In 1880, the territory had a population of 39,159 whites; by 1898, it was boasting a population of 142,924.

Joseph kept busy that summer and fall. He now had two hired hands, Charlie Randall and a new man, Tex Parker. Tex had a good sense of humor. "Pushed steers all the way from Texas, pushed cattle all over Montana. What am I doing now?

Kicking pigs in the ass. But at least I got a job. Mr. Gump, I don't have to ride and break them things?"

"One thing, Tex, you will learn fast. A pig is one smart animal and will play games with you."

A small bunkhouse had been built out by the barn, but the men still came in for meals, which were always plentiful. With both Mary and Emma as cooks, the food tasted good.

The men were all kept busy with the care of the stock that winter, which was mild for Montana. As the spring of 1899 arrived, things got busy again with the killing and preparing of the pork.

A new contract came in for Joseph. The Great Northern took over the Manitoba Railroad, which was in Central Montana and had 2,770 miles of track. The board of directors of a newly created Great Northern had voted to extend the railroad's lines westwardly from some suitable point in Montana to Puget Sound. The railroad would go from Havre over Marias Pass, down the middle fork of the Flathead River to Columbia Falls and Kalispell, and then turn northwest to follow the Kootenai River into the Idaho panhandle, passing through Spokane and crossing the Cascade Mountains to reach Everett, Washington, and on to Puget Sound by 1893.

The Great Northern Railroad would go past Joseph's property, and Joseph was to provide pork and beef to the railroad crew. He would raise or buy all the pork, beef, and mutton, then slaughter and prepare it for the railroad camps.

This was how the opportunity developed: no one could find a pass over the Rockies, and Jim Hill couldn't finish his railroad. The main problem was that between the Northern Pacific's crossing of the Rockies to the south and the Canadian Pacific's route to the north, there was no real pass through the mountains. Jim Hill needed to find a passage through the mountains lying due west from Havre in Northern Montana. The Indians and some whites had a legend about a pass through the Marias area, but it had been forgotten. In 1898, Jim Hill's location engineer, John F. Stevens, set out yet again to find the lost passage. In a blizzard, which was even too harsh for his Indian guide, Stevens walked into the lost Marias Pass. His discovery of Marias Pass opened the way to the Pacific, over the easiest crossing of the Northern Rockies.

CHAPTER TWELVE

JOSEPH ASKED MR. HOLLAND to become his partner in providing the beef and mutton and help him finance this venture. In 1899, Joseph Gump and Henry Holland became partners for providing meat to a hungry crew of railroad builders.

Mary hired people to help her in making sausage. The smokehouse had to be made larger, and wood had to be purchased for smoking the sausage. Emma was put in charge of the children, and Mary found herself heavily involved in their new enterprise.

It was a very profitable summer, and Mary and Joseph decided to buy a new house in the town of Havre. Joseph wanted to move his family from the farm and let his ranch hands move into the farmhouse and run the ranch. He wanted Mary and Emma in town, where they would have time to shop and go to church and be able to have friends.

The new home in town was a large four-bedroom house with a covered front porch on the main street. Although Mary was always sad to leave a place with all its fond memories, she also enjoyed making a new place hers. Yet she and Emma were still afraid that people would find out they were half-breeds. No one would ever know this looking at Mary or Emma, as they comported themselves with such self-respect and natural dignity. Most people thought that Mary and Emma were elegant women from the South, maybe New Orleans. Why people still carried that hatred for Indians and an even greater hatred for half-breeds, Mary couldn't understand.

Joseph opened a butcher shop in town for supplying the railroad camps and found a couple of good German butchers. People were coming from all over to buy his bacon, hams and sausage. Joseph was making a better living than he had expected, and his new partner was supporting any change he wanted to make.

The butcher shop was on Joseph's ranch, which was about three miles east of the town of Havre, where the railroads going North-South met the railroads going East-West, known as the division point for the Great Northern Railroad. It was also good to be a little ways from Havre. When cowpunchers, miners, and soldiers went to town all at one time, the townsfolk had to brace themselves or duck for cover. Havre could be one wild town.

It wasn't long before the area was known as "Pig Hill." This name didn't bother Joseph, as long as he was making a good living. Joseph was always able to find good help when he needed it, since he always treated everyone fair.

When Mary had any extra time, she would ask Joseph if she could try to trace her family because she knew so little about them. Joseph was always supportive and would go with her to the reservation or to any hall of records, as long as the trips were short so that he could keep track of his butcher shop.

One of the hardest things for Mary was not letting anyone— and it meant anyone—know she was part Indian. When people would ask her where she got her beautiful olive skin and dark eyes, she would say, "Oh, the French side of my family." The Indians, and especially the "half-breeds," were treated very badly in Montana.

Mary discovered that the American legal system, based on English common law precedents and American statute law oriented to white values, had never accommodated the different culture and status of the American Indian.

The mechanisms of the white man's law either were incapable of recognizing the cultural and legal separateness of the Indian or were deliberately designed to destroy the Indian's independence. As a result, if Joseph were to die, Mary still couldn't own his land or any of his property. The law wasn't clear as to whether her children, being quarter bloods, as they would be called, could inherit Joseph's property. Mary couldn't receive her mother's property on the reservation or Joseph's off the reservation. Under the white man's law, she didn't have the rights of either a white or an Indian

Joseph was always amazed at how bright Mary was, how logical her mind was, and how persistent she was. Mary was also one of the most protective and loving mothers he had ever seen. She gave her children the motherly love she had missed as a child.

Mary was able to get some information from the Tribal Agency. One document, "Who is an Indian?", made her shake her head:

"An Indian, legally and judicially, is defined in terms of his relationship to the Legal System of the United States, all Indians are noncitizens. Indians having recognized tribal status have rights and obligations on the reservation. A full-blooded Indian who has terminated or abandoned his tribal membership and has no claim to allotments or other benefits or obligations deriving from his tribal association is, for legal purposes, not an Indian. On the other hand, a member of a tribal unit, accepted as such by the tribe, though his Indian ancestry may be miniscule or tenuous, is, if accepted as an Indian by the tribal authorities and by the United States Governmental Agencies dealing with the Tribal Authorities. You are legally an Indian."

If Mary was accepted by the tribe and stamped "Approved" by the United States government, she would become a legal Indian and a noncitizen. The United States government didn't want anyone to exist in both worlds.

Mary was able to find some old 1880 United States census records, which proved that her father, her mother, and she herself did exist, and Maggie and the children were considered white Indians (whatever that meant).

#2433 Wells, James A. W. M.	46	Trader	Born: Indiana
" Magggie W.	F. 25	Keeping House	Born: Montana Indian
" LeRoy J. W.M.	9	Son:	Born: Montana Indian
" Wm. W. W.M.	6	Son	Born: Montana Indian
" Mary Le W.F.	4	Daughter	Born: Montana Indian
" Emma W.F.	2	Daughter	Born: Montana Indian

What amazed Mary was that she and her family were counted on the old U.S. Census records. All the males and females were considered "white Indians." It seemed as though the white United States government couldn't make up its mind when it counted the Indian population of Montana.

On August 5, 1900, Mary gave birth to a second son, named Merlin Joseph. That summer, the family also attended the wedding of Mary's brother William and his fiance, Flora, in Fort Benton. It was a fun visit, and both Mary and Emma enjoyed meeting Flora. Flora was good for William, who was still an accountant for T.C. Power.

Mary and Joseph helped William buy a house in Fort Benton. Mary tried hard to find their original home, but it had been many years since they had lived there. Here was another part of her history that was gone. While they were in Fort Benton, they tried to find Mr. Perkins, but his restaurant had been closed, and as far as they could learn, he had moved to Helena.

Mary and Joseph stayed at the Grand Union Hotel, which had just been remodeled and was now a beautiful place at which to stay. The hotel reminded them of their honeymoon. The staff tried hard to make the guests happy. Joseph said, "With all these rooms and so few guests, this place is going down again, but we get to see it in its splendor. So Mary, let's enjoy it!"

Mary was curious to find any mention of her father, but the only information was on T.C. Power, who was born in Dubuque, Iowa, in 1834 and who first entered Montana in 1864 as a civil engineer with a surveying party. T.C. Power had returned to Fort Benton in June of 1867, landing with a stock of goods on credit from Joseph Field, brother of the more noted Marshall Field. There wasn't a shack to be rented on the town's busy waterfront, but Isaac Baker loaned Power a large tent for the start of a firm that was to become Fort Benton's largest.

The first T.C. Power store was located at what they called the downriver corner of the block, which also held the Baker store. Additional stock came upriver on the Lady Grace in July. A brother, John W. Power, soon joined the firm, which became T.C. Power and Bro. It was John Power to whom Mary and Emma had to write when they needed clothes, shoes, or school supplies and to whom they had written when they wanted to see their mother. John Power was the one who had refused their request. He was also the one who had sold their home in Fort Benton. And he was the man William worked for in Fort Benton.

It was easy to find information on the T.C. Power enterprise. In 1868, their first joint enterprise, the Thwing house run by Miss Thwing, was started. The house was remodeled in 1874 and became the Chouteau House. The Powers wanted to become diverse in their enterprises. Their first freighting began in 1868. They opened a trading post at the Musselshell in 1864 against the possibility that the Fort Benton route would be bypassed. This is where Mary thought her father would be mentioned as the trader at the Musselshell, but not a mention was made of him. Mary's father had been erased from history. Although her father was an important part of Montana history, Mary couldn't find any mention of him anywhere.

Mary knew that her father had been a partner in the trading post and cattle ranch at the Judith. It was known that T.C. Power was trading on both sides of the Canadian boundary and he was known as a silent partner in the Canadian whiskey trade. Mary did find mention of John Healy, Joe Kipp, Fred Nanouse, John Kerler, and many others, but no Jim Wells.

T.C. Power was smart. He was the first Montana merchant to sense the coming of the growth of farming in the territory hard hit by exhaustion of placer mining. He set up farm implement agencies at Bozeman, Deer Lodge, and Virginia City in 1871 as well as in Helena. Within a year, he was bringing in one thousand dollars a day in farm implements alone.

Mary wanted to ask T.C. Power, "Is all that my father had gone? How is it that all your investments grew yet none of my father's grew?"

Joseph would look at Mary and say, "Mary, you must forget T.C. Power and what your father had. We are doing well and don't need him."

"I know, Joseph, but it isn't right for him to take all that belonged to us."

"He must live with what he has done. You have your family and a good future."

"You are right, Joseph. I do love you."

Now, many years later, Mary decided to make her first visit to John Power's office in Fort Benton to see him and the office her brother worked in.

John Power greeted Mary. He was happy to put a face with the name, since this was their first meeting. John Power was old and did not look well. Mary wondered how this old man had wielded such power in her life. Had she known what was on the other side of that pen, she would not have begged but would have demanded the things she had requested. Rather than ask, "May I please have a new pair of shoes, mine have many holes?" she would have stated, "I need shoes; send them. It's my money." or, "I'm going to see my mother; send me a ticket." John Power told her that T.C. Power was still a U.S. senator. Mary felt indifferent toward this old man who had simply been an instrument of his brother's designs.

Mary was anxious to leave Fort Benton but sad to say goodbye to William and Flora, but they all promised to get together for Christmas.

Traveling in Montana, Mary saw more and more farms. Joseph told her that the first farmers were the fur traders and missionaries. Vegetable gardens, crop fields, and grazing livestock surrounded such fur posts as Fort Benton and Connah. In the Bitterroot Valley, the Jesuit Priests began farming successfully in the 1840s. They imported seeds and domestic crops such as potatoes and wheat. The Jesuit Brothers even built the first crude flour mills. By the 1860s, a few isolated farmers were starting to till the soil. But it was the great gold rushes of the mid-sixties and the far-removed and hungry mining towns that grew up, along with their large demands for foodstuffs, that caused the farmers to start to respond to their demands. Joseph commented, "Just like my butcher shop and the railroad."

The placer gold towns of southwestern Montana, which always had food problems, had the most serious problems. Located four hundred miles to the south of them, the Mormon settlements in Utah eagerly welcomed the Montana trade. They could charge high prices; sometimes, winter and spring snowstorms blocked the roads. During the hard winter of 1864-1865, flour shortages in Virginia City drove the price of a hundred-pound sack of flour to one hundred fifty dollars; riots broke out as a result. The high price of food convinced many prospectors to give up mining and to start farming, since, coming from farming families, they knew farming.

Mary enjoyed hearing Joseph talk about the history of Montana. She was surprised, as were the pioneer farmers, that the high mountain valleys surrounding the gold fields were both richly fertile and well watered. Joseph had learned from the Jesuit Brothers that by selectively irrigating and carefully skirting the late spring and early autumn frosts, they could produce fine harvests of grain, vegetables, and even good fruits. Small farms were dotting the Jefferson, Rudy, Madison, Bitterroot, Deer Lodge, Prickly Pear, and other valleys along the continental divide. The broad Gallatin Valley was a real food producer and had three flour mills by 1867.

Farming was still limited, and the 1870 census listed only 851 farms and 150,000 cultivated acres. Montana was looking at ways to increase its farming. Joseph knew that the potential was there if they could control all the water that ran off the land, which he was doing by using the Milk River to grow extra hay.

In early fall, Mary was asked to teach some of the children in the area. She had the best education around and seemed to have a way with children. A small school was organized next door to the Catholic church. With Emma taking care of Marguerite, Leo, and Merlin, Mary set up the first school in that area. She had twenty-seven students, ages seven to fourteen years, and she enlisted a couple of mothers as helpers. The missions donated books.

Mary occasionally thought of telling her students that she was a half-breed, but she knew it would only cause problems for her family. It was still not uncommon to see an Indian shot in the streets. "The only good Indian is a dead Indian," continued to be the white man's motto.

William and Flora visited at Christmastime. Mary loved having her family around, and she seemed to glow. Flora was an easy person to have around and loved being with a family. William and Flora arrived a couple days before Christmas and joined Mary and Emma in the baking and other food preparations.

It was a busy time for the butcher shop. Joseph felt as though everyone in Montana wanted one of his hams and some of his bacon for Christmas.

"Just make sure you don't sell the two hams that are for us," Mary warned.

"I will bring them home early so they'll be safe. It seems like each year we have trouble keeping up with the demand for our smoked pork."

Mary was proud of her husband's business that he had started from scratch. "You really learned well from the Brothers," she told him.

"Thank you, Mary, but it has all been with your help."

It was the first Christmas that Marguerite was aware of all

the festivities. She frequently walked around calling loudly, "Uncle Willie, Aunt Flora!"

Mary would look down at her tiny daughter and say, "Marguerite, they are right here!"

Marguerite replied, "I know that, I like their names!"

And everyone would laugh.

Mary wanted to go to midnight mass. She had good memories of the midnight masses at the mission and sneaking those looks at handsome Joseph Gump.

The children were all bundled up. The boys slept through the ceremony, but Marguerite was all eyes, with all the decorations and candles. She was able to go up and see the crib scene. Mary told her, "That is Mary and Joseph, and in the crib is baby Jesus."

"Mother, you and Father are Mary and Joseph, but why am I not baby Jesus?"

"We are just lucky to have those good names, but Marguerite is the perfect name for you."

Marguerite responded simply, "Oh."

Christmas was fun with the children. Joseph made many of the toys: a dollhouse for Marguerite, a wooden horse for Leo, blocks for Merlin.

Mary made William and Joseph each a sweater; Emma made them each a scarf. Joseph made Mary a new kitchen table with six chairs, and he made Emma and Flora each a cedar chest. He also gave Emma and Marguerite a silver napkin ring. Mary was so excited as she retrieved the one that her mother had given her so many years before. All three were placed on the Christmas table. Mary felt as though her mother were present.

Joseph couldn't believe the Christmas dinner. The food just kept coming. Ham, potatoes, corn, cabbage, cornbread with honey-butter, and for dessert, pies, cake, cookies.

"Mary," Joseph told her, "you have enough food to feed the whole railroad crew, but I won't give any of it away."

Willie played his fiddle, and everyone danced.

Just before school started in January, Mary caught a cold that went into pneumonia. She became very sick, and Emma had to take over her class. Joseph was very worried, and the doctor warned him that Mary must be very careful with her health from now on. Since she had pneumonia once before, her lungs were damaged permanently. In fact, Mary would never fully recover from that last bout with pneumonia.

That summer Joseph received word that his stepfather had died and his mother was coming for a visit.

Caroline's visit was a wonderful one; Caroline helped Emma, since Mary was still weak and had developed some asthma. Caroline talked to Joseph about moving to Spokane where the air was drier and would be better for Mary. Joseph tried to explain to her that he was making a good living in Montana and didn't want to leave.

Montana was growing, but dry farming required large tracts of land, units big enough to allow for summer fallowing and for lesser crop yields per acre. The potential settler could either buy his land from realtors or railroads or get it free from the government. Ever since passage of the Homestead Act in 1862, the federal government had offered free farms to all American citizens. The Homestead Act provided the farmer with a quarter section of land, one hundred sixty acres, free except for a small filing fee. Then came a five-year "proving" period, and then the homesteader acquired full legal title to the land.

This original Homestead Act meant little to Montana, however, where one hundred sixty acres was far too little land for a family farm. The government realized that the Great Plains agriculture demanded larger acreages, so Congress passed several supplementary laws to provide more land to the homesteaders. One such law was the Desert Land Act of 1877, under which one could obtain a full 640-acre section of land for only $1.25 per acre if the owner improved the land for three years and irrigated part of it. This measure, which was pushed through Congress by organized stockmen, offered little hope to real farmers, who could seldom bear the costs of irrigation by themselves. Ranchers violated the law to gain grazing lands. Over three million acres of public lands in Montana passed into private hands under this Act. Mr. Hausner was able to increase his ranch under this Act, but Joseph wasn't interested, since he would have to move to get land next to his own property.

It was a hard autumn for Mary, who was still suffering from pneumonia from the previous winter. Often, as she did her usual chores, such as leaning over to pick up the children's toys or hanging out the wash, she found herself short of breath. Sometimes she would have coughing fits and would find droplets of blood on her hand. She felt a heavy pressure in her chest and dreaded the idea that her health should become a problem for the whole family. By late October, when the chill of winter grew near, Mary and Joseph decided that it would be good for Mary to go with the children and Emma to Spokane and spend the winter there with Joseph's mother.

The house was lonesome without Mary, Emma, and the children. Joseph went to Fort Benton for Christmas, but he told William and Flora, who was pregnant with their first child, "Since Mary is doing so much better in Spokane, I guess it is time I thought about leaving Montana."

Mary returned to Montana to spend the summer. One of her first side trips was back to the reservation in the hopes of finding any information about the part of her family that had been moved to Spokane so that she could try to contact them when she returned to Spokane. Then she could continue her family search out there.

At the office for the reservation, Mary told the woman her name.

"Mary Wells," said the woman. "I knew your mother. I have watched you come to the reservation wanting nothing more than to search for and find your family. I can help you. My name is Ruby Stiffarm. Please come with me." Mary followed Ruby down a hall to a room full of old boxes. Ruby walked right over to one of the boxes, said to Mary, "Look in here," and quietly left.

When Mary opened the box and took out the very first file, she nearly fainted when she saw the old reservation census records. The first one read:

1888 - Fort Belknap Agency

Gros Ventre and Assinabonis

June 20, 1888

Indian Name	English Name	Sex	Relationship	Age
128 1. *Maggie Wells*	*Maggie Wells*	F	*Wife*	34
2. *Tchi-Want*	*Capture*	M	*Husband*	37
3. *Le Wells*		M	*Son*	14
4. *William Wells*		M	*Son*	12
5. *James Wells*		M	*Son*	3
6. *Mary Wells*		F	*Daughter*	11
7. *Emma Wells*		F	*Daughter*	10

There were files and files full of old census records—1889, 1890, 1891, 1893, 1894, 1895—all there. Her mother, her brothers, her sister, and Mary herself, all were listed on every census record for the Gros Ventre Indians. Mary said to herself over and over, "Yes, Mother you are here on the rolls. I've found you!" She was deeply moved to see that her mother had never forgotten the children she bore from James Wells.

Then Mary found another record, the implications of which frightened her. Joseph, she, and their children were listed on the tribal records.

Indian Name/English Name	Relationship	Date of Birth	Sex
Gump, Joseph (White)	Husband	1867	M
Wells, Mary	Wife	1883	F
Margaret	Daughter	1896	F
Loe	Son	1898	M
Martin	Son	1900	M

"What should I do?" she whispered to Joseph. "Our children are on these records. Someone may try and take them away and force them to live on a reservation! The information must have come from John Power?"

Joseph took a hold of Mary's hand. "That can't happen, Mary. Don't be afraid."

Joseph understood Mary's fear. "Mary, you have always been proud of your mother. I understand why you are afraid. We will return to Spokane together and our children will not be treated by whites as Indians. But most of all, I want you to be proud of the beautiful person you are. We will tell the children about this one day. It will be the right thing to do."

In the records, the superintendent couldn't spell the names right, nor were the dates accurate. Martin for Merlin, Margaret for Marguerite, and they had Mary giving birth to Marguerite at the age of thirteen.

"They will never get anything right," Joseph went on. "You know this is the white man's way toward the Indian. It will go on forever."

Mary started to cry. "But Joseph, why?"

"Mary, the white man will take and take and never give until the Indians have nothing more that can be taken from them. My family left Germany because the government had to take all from its neighboring countries. As it seems, the United States government is taking all from the indigenous people. Just look at all the treaties with the Indians. Not one has been kept. My German government never kept any of its promises. Treaties just give governments more time to figure out how to take more and break the treaties."

"Joseph, it isn't fair."

"I know, Mary, but as you know, life isn't fair, especially if you are Negro or Indian. You have had good talks with Miss Fields. She is making the best of her life. So, Mary, must you with yours."

Mary was grateful to her husband for his wisdom, and didn't say a word all the way home to Havre.

CHAPTER THIRTEEN

HAVRE WAS GROWING every day, not just as a railroad hub but also as a thriving community, and Joseph's business was prospering. But Joseph knew he should be with his family. Spokane was also a good city and was becoming a railroad hub because of its lumber, minerals, wheat, livestock, and fruit, and Joseph was sure that he could make a good living there. Joseph figured that if he sold his butcher shop and leased out his farm, he would have enough money to move to Spokane and start over.

It was a difficult decision, but by July 1902, Joseph was on his way to eastern Washington. The Holland family took over the butcher shop, and Joseph leased his farm with the stock to an eastern hog farmer who knew the business. The agreement was that Joseph would get rent and part of the profit.

It was a wonderful homecoming for Joseph. Mary, Joseph's mother, Emma, and the children all greeted him with warm hugs. The children had grown so much. Joseph was more than glad to be back with his family after being away seven months.

"Mary, no more of these separations. I don't like them, and I hate cooking for myself."

"Is that all you missed—my cooking?"

"No, Mary, I missed you."

The trip to Joseph's mother's ranch had taken about an hour from Spokane. Caroline had forty acres on the edge of Spokane on a bluff that overlooked the Spokane River. She had a nice farm with fruit trees and a large vegetable garden, but the house had only three bedrooms. Even though it was crowded with all the visitors, everyone was happy to be together again.

Mary was feeling good. The drier climate was good for her breathing. She still had asthma attacks, but the doctors felt she was much better off in Spokane.

Joseph set out the morning after he arrived to look for a house and a job. That very morning he found a nice house with a large porch to rent that was near downtown and close to schools. It was an older home with four bedrooms—one for himself and Mary, one for Emma, one for Marguerite, and one for the boys. Joseph paid the owner two months' rent and arranged with the freight company to have their furniture shipped right to the house when it arrived from Montana on the freight wagon.

That evening, everyone was surprised to hear that he had found a house so quickly. Joseph explained that the furniture would arrive in about two weeks, which would give them time to paint the house and clean it up. Every morning for the next week, Joseph, Mary, and Emma worked on the house. They all loved it and were pleased that they would have a place of their own again. By the end of August, the furniture had arrived, a little the worse for the long ride in the wagon, bumping and scratching all the way, but nothing Joseph couldn't fix.

Marguerite was registered at Bancroft School. When Mary came home from registering her daughter, she said, "Joseph, Spokane is wonderful. No one cares what you are; everyone is equal. I'm sorry we had to leave Montana, but I think Spokane will be good for our family."

"So you are pleased with the school?"

"Oh, yes. Marguerite will do well here. The school has everything. You can't believe what they have for the children. They will even take Leo in preschool to give him a good start."

"Tomorrow I must start looking seriously for a job."

"Joseph, you have so much to offer. You won't have a problem."

The next day Joseph saw an ad in the paper: "Spokane Fire Department expanding and opening new stations. Needs good men with horse experience."

"Mary, what would you think if I became a fireman?"

"Is that something you would like?"

"I think I would be good. I sure know my horses."

Joseph put on his suit and went down to the central firehouse to get an application. The man at the desk handed Joseph the sheet of paper. "Sure hope you know your horses. No one seems to around here."

"I sure do. I'm from Montana," Joseph replied.

The fire commander had heard Joseph through his open door and immediately ordered the man at the desk to "send that fellow from Montana in here right now."

"Yes, sir."

The commander held out his hand as he introduced himself to Joseph.

"I'm Joseph Gump."

"Mr. Gump, what brings you to Spokane?"

"My mother lives here, and my wife had some health problems. We were advised to move here."

"Mr. Gump, you want a job as a fireman?"

"Yes, sir, I do."

"You know horses and horse teams?"

"Yes, sir."

"I like you, Mr. Gump. Tell the lieutenant to give you employment papers. You pass the physical, you have the job."

"Thank you, Sir."

Joseph filled out the papers and made an appointment for a physical the next day. He was so excited he could hardly wait to get home.

"Mary—Mary—Emma, where are you?"

"You are like Marguerite—we're right here," Mary called from the kitchen. "What is all the excitement?"

"Mary, I think I have a job as a fireman. All I have to do is pass the physical tomorrow."

Joseph was up early the next morning. He was very anxious. "Joseph, your physical isn't until 2 p.m."

"I know it, but I just couldn't sleep. I would really like to try this work."

Joseph was at the doctor's office forty-five minutes early. When he finally heard his named called, he went in to see the doctor. Joseph removed his clothes, and the doctor examined him from head to toe.

"Mr. Gump, you appear to be in perfect health, and your body is that of a man who isn't afraid of work. The one observation I have is that you must have had poor nutrition as a child. See your breastbone, how it comes out to a point?"

"Yes, it's always been that way. Will it give me any problems?"

"No, but we just don't see many individuals with chests like yours. You have what is called a 'chicken breast' Mr. Gump, I will send all your papers over to the firehouse. I don't think a chicken breast should stop you from being a good fireman."

Joseph told Mary and Caroline, who was visiting, his good

news. "The only thing about me was my 'chicken breast,' as the doctor called it. He said it was from poor food when I was a baby."

Caroline growled, "You had very good food as a baby! That is the way you were born. Ach! What a thing to say."

Two days later, Joseph received a letter from the fire commander asking him to report to the firehouse. That very afternoon, Joseph was hired. The following week, a training class was formed, and Joseph was the last in the group to be included. Joseph was very proud of his job and pleased that he had found it so quickly.

The training was hard, but Joseph learned a lot, from how to pump water and carry people down ladders to driving a team of horses.

On graduation day, Joseph Gump's whole family attended the ceremony. Mary was very proud. Joseph looked so handsome in his new uniform. He introduced his family to his classmates and the commander. Joseph received a special citation for finishing at the top of his class and for being the best handler of the horse team. Even before he started work, he was given a promotion. He would be driving the horses.

Joseph loved his work. In his spare time, he was able to make many new pieces of furniture for the house.

The family settled into their new house. The great feature about the firehouse was that it held a family dance every Saturday night with food served at midnight. The whole family looked forward to these dances, and Mary and Joseph were among the most spirited of the dancing couples.

One day, as Joseph was looking in the phone book, he wondered whether there were other people in town named Gump. He found one man named Collier Gump and telephoned him. The two men could find no common relatives in their conversation, but Joseph invited Collier for Sunday dinner. He told Mary that he had invited a guest for dinner Sunday night whom he knew nothing about except that he was a Gump."

When Sunday came around, a handsome young man in his early twenties arrived at the door with flowers for Mary. The dinner conversation was around each of their families. Collier wasn't married, and he worked for the city of Spokane as an engineer. He and Emma really seemed to hit it off. As Collier was leaving, Joseph invited him to the firehouse dance the following Saturday.

"Emma, what do you think of Collier?" Mary asked her sister.

"He seems nice. But he has that funny last name, Gump, and I have always told you I would never want that as my last name."

In the spring of 1903, Emma and Collier were married and moved into their own home. At last, Emma had her own home, even though it meant having to be Emma Gump.

That same spring, Mary received word from her brother William that he and Flora were getting a divorce and that Flora and their son Victor were moving to Tacoma, Washington. This was a real shock to Mary, who had never known anyone who was divorced. She couldn't understand how anyone in her family could do such a thing! Mary loved Flora and believed she was good for William. She knew the problem had to be with William.

A couple of days later, Mary received a letter from Flora stating that William had developed a terrible drinking problem. No matter how hard she had tried, nothing seemed to work with him. The only thing she felt she could do to save herself and Victor was to get a divorce and move to Tacoma. She hoped that Mary and Joseph would understand and be part of her family.

Mary then received a third letter—this one from the T.C. Power Company—stating that William had a bad drinking problem that was having an adverse effect on his work and that they were worried about him.

Mary spoke to Joseph, who was supportive of Mary and told her they should try to get William to move to Spokane where they felt they could get him some help.

Mary wrote to William and asked him to stop his drinking and move to Spokane so that he could be close to family. She felt he could get a job easily in Spokane as an accountant.

William wrote back to Mary saying that things weren't too good since John W. Power had died in 1901. The rest of the Power family were just maintaining a sort of proprietary interest in Fort Benton. Also, with the loss of Flora and his son, William didn't have any ties to Fort Benton, which had become a lonesome place for him. There was still a lot of bad feeling at the company, since he was now the senior accountant yet everyone called him a half-breed behind his back. He agreed with Mary and said he would settle his affairs and move to Spokane.

One cold night in November, just over a year after they had moved into the rented house, a fire started in a crack in the chimney. Joseph was on call at the firehouse, and Mary awoke to the smell of smoke. She began to cough and ran frantically to the other bedrooms and gathered up the sleeping children. The fire spread so fast that by the time the firemen arrived, they were able to save only some rugs, one painting of Mary's, and a few odds and ends. Joseph was among the firefighters who arrived to save his own house. He actually cried to think of losing all of Mary's paintings that she had made at the mission as well as all his handmade furniture. Mary was just as sad about Emma's needlework.

"I couldn't even save my own house," Joseph kept saying.

"It happened so fast, Joseph. No one could have saved it."

The children stood outside in their nightgowns crying, especially Marguerite, since all but the one doll she was holding in her arms were in the house. A sympathetic little neighbor girl named Sally came over and put her arm around Marguerite. "Don't cry," she said. "I will give you some of my dolls."

Joseph put his arms around Mary and the children and said, "Don't worry about the things. I just thank God you are all safe."

Neighbors lent them blankets, and Mary and Joseph bundled all the children up and put them into the wagon. Joseph rode them out to Grandma Caroline's house. When Joseph's mother saw them arriving, all huddled together in the wagon in the dawn light, she was so frightened she started calling out in German. "It's okay, Mother, we're all right. It's okay now," Joseph yelled to his mother in German.

Joseph and Mary went right out that day and found a house they could afford to buy. With the help of all the firemen, the house was painted and cleaned, and with donated furniture, they were able to move in within a week. Emma and Collier were a huge help, too. Emma promised to help sew new curtains and pillows, and even make dollclothes for Marguerite.

Later that year, Emma and Collier had a baby named Ursula, and Mary and Joseph became her godparents.

"Ursula Gump, what a name," Joseph teased Emma.

William moved to Spokane that summer. He stayed with Grandma Caroline out on her farm. They got along well, and he was good company to her. Collier was able to get William a job as an accountant where he worked—at the Washington Water and Power Company.

The family settled into life in Spokane. Everybody's favorite event was still the Saturday night dance. William would come into town with Grandma, and sometimes he'd dance with little Marguerite.

Joseph moved right up in the ranks. By 1910, he was a lieutenant in the Spokane Fire Department and had his own station.

Mary still had a hard time getting Joseph to talk about his family, but Caroline was always eager to talk. Joseph was born in a small village in Germany called Oberkreutzberg, in Bohemia. Caroline's family, the Wallners, had small farms and were also wood carvers. Caroline had married Joseph's father against the wishes of her family, since the Gumps weren't as wealthy as the Wallners. Caroline received a settlement from her family.

Joseph was born a year later on March 23, 1869. When Joseph was eight years old, Joseph's family left Germany. They could see no future in Germany, since all Germany was doing was fighting wars with Frederick William IV, who had become regent for his insane brother William the First. Then Frederick William IV had become the King of Prussia in 1861. His reign was dominated by Bismarck, whom he appointed chancellor in 1862. Bismarck took personal command in the Franco-Prussian war, at the conclusion of which he was proclaimed Emperor of Germany. All Caroline and Joseph Sr. could see ahead of them was more wars and the potential of their son dying as a young soldier, so they decided to come to America in 1878.

Caroline's sister, Anna Wallner, came with them. They all settled first in Milwaukee, where Joseph Sr. worked in a brewery as a brewmaster. Joseph Sr. had children by Anna, which greatly upset Joseph Jr. Somehow, though, it was all right with Caroline, who figured that Anna, who didn't speak English, probably wouldn't have married.

After a period in Milwaukee, Joseph Sr. was offered a job in Spokane at a small brewery and moved the family there. He died a year later, and Anna and her children moved to Sacramento, California, where Anna died in 1910.

Caroline remarried a man named Mr. Sapper, who had two children. Joseph couldn't stand his stepfather and moved to Montana. Despite Joseph Sr.'s second family, Joseph who had a close relationship with his father and would have preferred that his mother, Caroline, had remained a widow. Caroline kept close contact with Anna's children, the "California relations."

Mary felt that her own children couldn't have made her happier. Marguerite was very bright and outgoing and very eager to work hard at whatever she tried; and Leo, though more introverted than his sister, was extremely intelligent and hard-working. Merlin was the only one of her children who gave her any trouble. Somehow he had the desire to wander, and when he was ten years old, he left home for no apparent reason. Mary and Joseph had everyone looking for him. After searching all day, Mary woke Marguerite at night, and they looked up and down the streets, but no matter what they did they couldn't find him.

One day, William came over to Mary and Joseph's house wanting to speak to Mary. Mary made a pot of coffee, and she and her brother sat at the kitchen table.

"You, Mary," William started in, "of all the people I know, should be able to understand your child Merlin. You should see that he still has the soul of an Indian in a white man's world. You must watch him and listen to him and understand what is calling him. You must understand his visions."

Mary's mind flashed way back to a time that was almost lost. She could hear her mother saying, "A true Indian does not have dreams; he has visions, and he who has visions is special."

Mary was surprised, since she had never heard William speak about his Indian past.

Was Merlin special? All Mary could think about was the loss of her child, a child who was different and, yes, a dreamer.

Mary knew she was losing all contact with her Native American heritage. The thing she wanted to save most was moving into her past; the thing she had promised to cherish was vanishing. She, of all people, should know that her son was protected by special spirits and the grandfathers. But could she, Mary, fully accept this? Was she being tested? She had no answers to any of her own questions. She was sickened with worry. After five weeks, Merlin returned.

"Merlin, where have you been? Why did you do this?"

"Mom, I do not know. I felt that I must go, and I did not know where I was going, but I felt I must go. I got as far as Salt Lake and knew it was time to come home."

"Please, if you ever feel like running away again, just let us know where you are. I have been sick over you being gone."

"Mom, I can't explain the feeling. I just felt and knew I must go, and I walked off." Merlin described how he would stop at houses for food and ride on the railroad boxcars. Finally, tired of traveling, he had told a conductor he had to get back to his sister's wedding, and the conductor gave him new clothes and a ticket to Spokane.

Merlin was so different from Leo and Marguerite, who were quiet, studious children who never caused any problems.

In fact, Mary and Marguerite eventually did everything together, since Joseph worked long hours at the firehouse. Mary was used to having one close female to rely on. First it had been her mother, then Miss Fields, then Emma, and now Marguerite.

Mary and Emma taught Marguerite how to embroider, and the three of them spent hours sitting and talking and doing needlework. It was good for Marguerite, since it was during this time that she heard many of the stories about the mission and her mother and Aunt Emma's early life there. But when Marguerite asked her mother and her aunt about life before the mission, they found it hard to talk about.

Emma's embroidery work was beautiful. Mary would say to her, "Emma, you have the best fingers for this work."

"No, Mary, I have more patience," she would reply.

Both Mary and Emma often wrote to the mission Sisters, but the mission had burned down, and a new school and convent had been built in Great Falls. The sister who kept the closest contact with them was Mother Elizabeth, who would send cards and remember every birthday.

On Leo's eleventh birthday—July 14, 1911—Joseph brought home a little pitbull for him that they named Jeff. The first thing they did was have the dog's ears clipped, which was done to make the ears stand up. Jeff was a great dog and was loved by everyone in the neighborhood. He wouldn't leave Leo's side. Leo loved coming home from the store or from school and having this happy dog there to greet him.

Also in the summer of 1911, Joseph had to take a leave from the fire department and go back to Montana to fix up his farm to sell it. The whole family went to Montana and stayed with the Holland family while Joseph tried to get the ranch back into shape to sell.

It was fun for the children to spend a summer on a big ranch, but Mary took them back to Spokane in the fall, and Joseph stayed the winter in Montana. It was another year before the ranch was sold, but this made for two summers when the family could enjoy Montana.

The thing they remembered most was rounding up the cattle and branding the calves, then putting them in a pen and running the mother cows off. The mothers would stand around and bawl on one side of the fence with the calves bawling on the other side. Finally, the mothers would grow hungry and start wandering away, and the calves could hear their mother's cry getting farther off. When you have thousands of bawling animals, the noise can be overwhelming.

Marguerite had a friend named Virginia Houser who was almost blind and had to wear thick glasses. Virginia had moved with part of her family to Lake Chelan in eastern Washington. Marguerite was allowed to spend summers with her. She would tell her mother that the Housers were like second parents to her.

Lake Chelan was beautiful country, with many farms and apple orchards. Virginia's father had died, and the ranch was being run by Virginia's mother and Aunt Nettie. Marguerite was always impressed by their house, a small house at the end of the lake. The floors were plain planks, but they had a shine in which you could see yourself. And the table was always set with a white linen tablecloth and napkins. Oh, how Virginia hated to iron those fancy tablecloths. The ranch was ten miles from the nearest town. Apples were its main crop, but Nettie raised potatoes that were sold in the area. The potatoes were the best around, dense and moist, and were known as "Nettie's gems."

Marguerite had her first experience riding a horse at Lake Chelan. Virginia was a good rider, but since her sight was so bad, she always had to have someone with her. She and Marguerite rode around the lake. Marguerite was so sore she couldn't sleep or walk the next day.

When Marguerite was twelve years old, Mary and Joseph moved to a bigger house. The beautiful home was located at East 213 7th Avenue, an address that would, they all hoped, represent their last move.

Just as they were settling into the new home, Merlin left home again. He was eleven years old, and again the family was frantic. At least this time Merlin did send a card from Salt Lake and one from Wyoming. He was gone almost six months when he was picked up as a runaway and sent home.

Mary and Joseph would talk to him for hours trying to find out why he would leave. He would just say, "I get this feeling to just go, and I go."

Around Christmas, while Merlin was still away, Mary and Joseph found Jeff outside lying on the lawn dead. The dog had been poisoned. It was terrible, and Mary cried and cried, as did Leo and Marguerite. Joseph made a little box for Jeff and buried him in the backyard. The loss of Jeff was the hardest thing for Merlin when he returned home.

Mary woke up each day worrying that Merlin would be gone again. "Mary," Joseph would say, "if he is going to go, all we can do is make a welcome home for him when he comes back. He must feel he is always welcomed at home and loved."

"But why, Joseph?" Mary responded, worried.

"Mary, no one knows why someone is a wanderer."

Marguerite made her first communion that year. She wore a new white dress, and the family all came to celebrate. It was a wonderful day for Marguerite, although it was marred by the death of one of the young girls in her class about three weeks before first communion day. The Sisters told the group, "We all miss Anne, but she is with us looking down from heaven this day." A special prayer was offered at the ceremony for her. At home that afternoon, Marguerite received presents from everyone in her family. Money from her parents, a prayer book from Grandma Gump, a rosary from Emma, a book from Uncle Willie. It was fun seeing the whole family together.

It seemed as if a lot happened that year. Caroline became

very sick and moved into town with Mary and Joseph. Shortly after, the doctors discovered she had stomach cancer, and she lived only six more months. Mary and Joseph were crushed, but Caroline left her children and grandchildren many happy memories of her taking them in her buggy on the ten-mile ride to her farm. Caroline would always stop at a little store on the way to buy the children a treat and a can of beer for herself. She had a large strawberry bed and would pick and sell the berries for grocery money. The children would spend hours in the strawberry patch picking and eating berries. It was quite a picture to see—this small German woman hoeing and caring for her garden and, when she became tired, leaning on her hoe. Caroline was a wonderful woman and was missed by everyone.

Mary often teased Caroline. "Grandma, what are you going to do in heaven with more than one husband?"

Caroline would get a big smile. "Ah, those devils will be in hell."

"Grandma, that isn't nice."

"Oh," she would say with her German accent, "but it is true."

Just before Caroline died, Marguerite saw her standing in front of her bedroom mirror wearing her robes from the third order of St. Francis. Her arms were crossed.

"Grandma, what are you doing?"

"I want to see what I will look like in my coffin."

"Grandma, that is terrible."

"No, Marguerite, it is good I'm ready. It is good."

When Marguerite saw her grandmother in her robes in the casket, she did look just like she had looked posing in front of the mirror.

CHAPTER FOURTEEN

MARY WAS VERY PROUD of Marguerite and Leo, who both continued to do well in school and who both had many friends. Merlin was still a problem, a dreamer at school with that wanderlust. As the teachers said, "Very bright, but a dreamer." Mary and Joseph always feared each day that he would just disappear again. After a while, Joseph began to feel that this constant fear was having an effect on Mary's health. The more nervous Mary became, the more asthma attacks she had. Some nights she would cough all night and could hardly breathe. The doctors said she should move to California, somewhere like Sacramento where it's hot and dry. They also told her that worry can cause asthma.

Even though they were mother and daughter, Mary and Marguerite were good friends and enjoyed doing things together. Mary felt she was very blessed to have so much and to live free of the prejudices that were held in Montana. Mary would become like a little girl when she and her daughter went shopping or out to lunch together. But the most fun they had was at the dances.

In the summer, Joseph took another leave from the fire department to help run the Holland ranch in Montana. Mr. Holland wanted to take his family back to Germany for a visit. He had written to Joseph that he couldn't trust his ranch in anybody else's hands but Joseph's and that he would pay Joseph very well if he would please come. Joseph believed it was a great opportunity for his family to spend time again in Montana. He took Leo and Merlin with him in early summer, and Mary and Marguerite followed later.

That summer, Mary took Marguerite and Merlin to the reservation to see whether she could find anything about her brother James and her half-brothers and half-sisters. She was not treated very well this time, however, and wasn't given any information. Mary had the reservation records pulled, and she, Emma, William, Lee Roy, and James were all on the tribal rolls. Mary told the people at the reservation that since she was on the records, she was entitled to information about her mother and her mother's second family. She was told that all records were in boxes. "Please come back in five years," they said. "Maybe we can find entitlement records."

Mary and her children went on down to the town of Hayes, on the grounds of the Reservation, where St. Paul's Mission was. The mission was still run by the Ursulines, and the church had been completed. The church, which had been established through the hard work of Brother Caroignano, whom Mary knew, was beautiful. Mary was told that it was the gem and pride of the entire region. The government had withdrawn all school subsidies in 1900, but St. Paul's had carried on successfully with the help of many friends and the Catholic Indian Bureau in Washington. The Sisters were so proud of their boarding school, which had more than one hundred students.

It was still a discouraging day, not being able to get any information. When Mary and her children tried to find Mary's mother's grave, they could find no trace at all of where it had been. Even the little cross was gone. Mary sat down in the weeds right in the middle of the cemetery and started to cry. Marguerite and Merlin had never seen her cry like that before.

"It is okay, Mother. She is in heaven. Please don't cry, please."

"I'm okay, Marguerite. She was such a wonderful woman and was treated so badly just because she was an Indian."

"Mother, where is Grandpa buried?"

Mary clearly remembered that day long ago, but all of that part of her life felt as if it had happened to somebody else. "My mother and all of us children took him out and buried him along the bank of the Missouri River. But remember, Marguerite, I was only a little girl. They took us from our mother and put us in the mission school."

Just then, Father Mackin walked out into the cemetery. "Is everyone okay?"

With tears running down her face, Mary looked at him. "No, Father, I can't find my mother. I need to tell her I love her."

Father Mackin took Mary's hand. "She knows you love her, and she doesn't need to be here anymore. She is with you and your family now."

Mary took her children in her arms. "I only wish you could have known her. She was a beautiful, gentle, loving mother. Her only problem was that she was Indian, and an Indian couldn't keep her children in this country. The blacks had it hard as slaves. But Indians couldn't own anything, and the United States government tried to destroy every Indian like they did the buffalo. It is hard to say you are Indian, and you will not be able to, but in your heart be proud."

As they rode back through the reservation, Mary said, "Just look, children, what they have done to a proud people."

It was a good summer, even if it was a sad summer for Mary. The family always enjoyed spending time at the Holland ranch. While Mary was at the ranch, she would try to learn all of Anne Holland's German recipes so that she could cook them for Joseph back in Spokane. The only thing was that Anne Holland cooked for all the ranch hands, and Mary had a hard time figuring out how to cut down the huge recipes for a family the size of hers.

One thing Mary did that summer was to arrange to meet Miss Fields in Great Falls. Joseph looked forward to the trip, since it was always fun for him to see Mary and Miss Fields together. The two women would talk and laugh for hours about their time at St. Peter's Mission. Miss Fields was getting very old and was having trouble moving around. She told Mary and Joseph that she was still allowed in any of the bars and saloons around Cascade and Great Falls.

The three of them made a point while in Great Falls to visit the Sisters at the Ursuline convent. It was hard for Mary, since she knew only Mother Elizabeth. Miss Fields knew everyone, since she had delivered their mail at St. Peter's Mission until it burned down.

Mary and Joseph tried to talk Miss Fields into coming to Spokane for a visit, especially during the cold winter months. Miss Fields told them she wasn't going any farther west and that she wanted to be buried at Cascade out on the trail, like Mary's father.

Mary told Miss Fields that she felt she had let her mother down since she had moved to Spokane, since all her Indian heritage was vanishing. Her children showed very little interest, and her family had become, as she put it, "very white."

Miss Fields laughed. "I'm not part of my black heritage, but as you can see, I will always be black—Black Mary—to everyone around here. Just support your family and don't worry about your past. Your past can only hurt you. You must live for the future and your beautiful family."

Mary told Miss Fields that she didn't want to lose her past. Miss Fields told Mary that her past was lost when she was sent to St. Peter's Mission and taken away from her family. The same thing had been done to her own family when the family members were taken and sold. In this way, families and traditions are destroyed, and one's past is gone and can't be found no matter how hard one tries. Mary told Miss Fields that all this made her very angry. Miss Fields asked Mary who she could be mad at, since you can't be mad at the whole world. Miss Fields took Mary in her arms and said to her, "Mary, as I said to you, please let go and move on."

Mary always found it hard to say good-bye to Miss Fields, who was truly like a mother to her. On the way back to Havre, Joseph told Mary that he didn't think Miss Fields would last much longer. Miss Fields was showing her age, and Montana was a hard place for a single woman to live.

Mary said to Joseph, "She may be getting old, but I will bet you she can still beat the best man in Montana to the draw, and I don't think you can find a man in Montana who will take a chance against her."

"You are right, Mary. She is one very tough woman. I will always love and respect her."

When the family had returned to Spokane and Marguerite's fourteenth birthday rolled around, Mary and Joseph wanted to do something very special. Mary found a beautiful ivory dresser set that had all the extra pieces: picture frame, comb and brush, clothes brush, powder box, and tray. It was one of the most beautiful ivory sets Mary had ever seen. The store engraved Marguerite's initials—M.H.G.—on each piece in old English script at no charge. It was the best present that Mary and Joseph could have ever given her, and it took a place of honor on her dresser.

That fall, the children all attended Lewis and Clark High School. Because she wanted to graduate early, Marguerite carried a heavy load. Mary kept telling her to enjoy high school, not to rush, but Marguerite kept taking six subjects. She would eventually finish high school in three and a half years.

Mary's brother William, who had stayed on at Caroline's farm after Joseph's mother died, was found dead at the farm. William had been found by a friend who played cards with him every day. The sheriff said that he must have had a heart attack. Mary and Joseph had a small Catholic ceremony for him, and he was buried next to Joseph's mother. Joseph thought that since they had become friends in life, they could play cards together at the cemetery.

The second bad news was in a letter from Mother Elizabeth. Miss Fields had died and, at her request, had been buried out on the trail between Cascade and St. Peter's Mission. A very large wake was held at the saloon in Cascade. Miss Fields had paid for it in advance.

It was hard for Mary to realize that Miss Fields was gone. The death of the woman who had been like a mother to Mary would leave a big empty spot in Mary's heart. Joseph took Mary in his arms and said, "Mary, I must smile. She went out the way she wanted, and she was still a scandal to the Sisters at the Ursuline convent. I'm sure that none of the Sisters were at the wake."

Mary had to smile, too. "She was one great special woman who had a lot to do with my life."

The next three and a half years seemed to go so fast for Mary. All of a sudden it was graduation time for Marguerite. Since she was graduating in January, she wouldn't be able to graduate with her class. She was only seventeen years old and wouldn't be eighteen until September.

Against Mary's wishes, Marguerite took the two-day teacher's exam and passed it with ease. Mary still felt that Marguerite was pushing herself and was missing the best part of her senior year in high school. No sooner had she taken the test than she was offered a job. A school had lost a teacher up in Kettle Falls, Washington, about eighty miles north of Spokane. Marguerite accepted the position and was soon off to a new experience. This was very hard on Mary, since it was the first time the two of them would be separated for any length of time.

From the very first day, Marguerite missed her mother and wrote to her every day telling her of her every experience. Mary would wait for these letters and read them to Joseph at dinner.

The school was a shock. Kettle Falls had only a one-room school, and Marguerite was given all the students, from first grade to eighth grade. Teaching was going to be a challenge to her—only seventeen and her first time away from home.

Marguerite was to board, for twenty dollars a month, with a family named Haig who had four children: a boy about twenty years of age who had arthritis and was in a wheelchair, a girl about fourteen (who was almost as old as Marguerite and, as she said, much wiser), and two younger boys. The school was a couple of miles away, and they all had to walk to school, although in the winter they got a buggy ride. In the winter, someone had to build a fire ahead of time in the stove so that the school would be warm when they arrived. This didn't always happen, however, and many times Marguerite had to build her own fire and wait until the room warmed up before she could start class.

Everyone was kind to Marguerite, since she was the only teacher around. Marguerite always enjoyed Saturday nights. Everyone in the area would go to the Grande Hall to dance all night, and food would be served at midnight. The children would be wrapped up and would be seen sleeping everywhere along the walls. At dawn, people would stagger off to church, and then they'd sleep most of Sunday.

While Marguerite was staying with the Haig family, the Haigs purchased a Ford, the first car in the entire area and the first Marguerite had ever been in. The Haigs had a bathtub in the house, but since it wasn't connected, everyone took a bath in a wash basin in his or her own room. Mr. Haig had money, but he was so cheap that every night he allowed only one lamp to burn between the kitchen and the dining room, and everyone was to use this one lamp. Marguerite would sit at the dining room table writing lesson plans, and the children would sit nearby doing homework and reading. Mr. Haig would take his wife Mabel across the lake once a week to Kettle Falls to buy groceries. Every other week, he would bring back a nickel's worth of candy for the children.

Mary was worried when Marguerite wrote that she had a boyfriend from Kettle Falls and was taking him to the dances. But Marguerite told her mother they were just good friends. Then Marguerite wrote about going to John's house for dinner and meeting his family. She said the family was surprised to learn that she was a Catholic. She was the first Catholic they had ever met, and she had the impression they were surprised that she didn't have horns on her head. She eventually became friends with his family, who accepted her as a human. She and John would laugh about his parents' reaction to her.

Marguerite spent a year in Kettle Falls. Then she received a scholarship at the Norman School at Holy Names Academy in

Spokane, and she moved home. This was also the year that her brother Leo was accepted at the Colorado School of Mines. Leo wanted to become a mining engineer. Merlin was still at home and a worry to the family. Mary would say, "If only I can get him through high school—one more year."

Mary was happy to have Marguerite home. The teaching program that was run by Holy Names Academy in Spokane was an excellent one, and many of the teachers in the area had graduated from it. Marguerite felt that she was having an easier time, since she had already taught for a year. Even so, she was learning so much more, which would make teaching easier.

The year that Marguerite was apart from her family had brought Mary and Marguerite even closer. Marguerite was an adult now, and she and her mother had many wonderful talks. The only thing Marguerite missed was her paycheck, which had been 80 dollars.

The two years at Holy Names went fast for Marguerite. Just before her graduation in June, the country entered into war when the United States declared war on Germany on April 6, 1917. All the young men were volunteering for the service. Everyone hoped it would be a short war. Leo wouldn't be called up, since he was in college; Merlin had left home again, and no one knew where he was. Mary said to Joseph, "Maybe Merlin's wandering has been for the good."

As soon as Marguerite graduated, she was offered a job at Coeur D'Alene, Idaho, only fifty miles from Spokane. This meant that she could get home for all the holidays. Again, she was given a small school—a one-room school where she was not only the teacher but also the janitor.

Marguerite lived with the Harder family on their cattle ranch. The family was having a hard time, since they were German and people were treating Germans badly. It reminded

Marguerite of how her grandmother, Maggie Wells, had been treated.

The Harders were wonderful people, and Marguerite loved Anna Harder. The two women would spend hours chatting on the front porch swing. Marguerite learned that Mr. Harder had sent to Germany for Anna, who knew nothing about him except that he was a rich American cattleman. Anna was surprised when Mr. Harder brought her out into the country—bare and isolated, with no neighbors for miles.

The Harders had three children: a seventeen-year-old son, a twelve-year-old son, and a young daughter. The younger son had only one arm. He had been hunting with his father and had set his gun on the boat. When he jumped into the boat, the shotgun went off, hitting him just above the elbow, blowing his arm off. Having only one arm didn't slow him down, and he could still do all his chores.

It was a happy year for Marguerite, though uneventful, since they lived so far away from everything.

Marguerite spent the summer at home with her family. In the fall, she was transferred to another school in Coeur d'Alene, Idaho. She was assigned to teach only fifth and sixth grades. Marguerite was placed in a small boarding house with another teacher, Amy Melville. The two of them became friends from the day they met. Their main complaint was that there were no men around. Since all the men were off to war, Marguerite and Amy would spend hours knitting socks and sweaters for the soldiers overseas.

The woman who ran the boarding home was a dear woman who had a very, very old aunt who lived in the house. At mealtime, the aunt would say a long grace, with the skin under her chin wobbling from side to side like an old turkey. Marguerite and Amy would pass up many meals to avoid the long, wobbling, turkey-neck grace.

In November of 1918 the war ended. It had been an expensive war for the world, with an estimated 10 million lives lost and 20 million people wounded. But it was supposed to be the war to end all wars, and everyone was to put his or her trust in the newly formed League of Nations. The men who had survived would be coming home soon.

Marguerite wrote her parents about the terrible principal the school had. The principal was an old woman who was jealous of the younger teachers. On Halloween, the teachers had a dance for the students to keep them out of trouble. The teachers were teaching the children how to dance, and everyone was having fun. The next morning, the townspeople found an outhouse on the school porch and a buggy on the roof of the local store. The school's boys weren't in on the prank, but the school principal was upset that the women had danced with the "little boys," saying that "it wasn't healthy."

Marguerite looked the principal right in the eye and said, "They had a lot of fun and didn't get into trouble. I do see that the older boys put a new office for you on the front porch." The principal told Marguerite that she was going to give Marguerite a poor evaluation. Marguerite told her that was all right with her, since one year with the principal was all she could handle.

At the end of the year, a party was given for Marguerite and Amy. The whole town attended, except the principal. Many wrote letters of recommendation for the two teachers, who were told they'd be greatly missed. The young teachers both had jobs waiting for them in Burke, Idaho.

Amy went home with Marguerite that summer, and they went to Montana to spend some time with the Hollands while Joseph helped them for a couple of months. Amy, Mary, and Marguerite had a wonderful time going to dances with the cowhands.

Having Marguerite and Amy in Montana for the summer made for a happy summer for Mary, but one that went too fast. Both Marguerite and Amy were anxious to start their new teaching jobs in Burke, Idaho, even though they didn't have the slightest idea where it was or what it looked like. They took the train from Spokane to Wallace, Idaho, then another train up to Burke. What a surprise for these two city girls!

The town of Wallace had been founded by a Colonel Wallace, who had discovered silver. By 1887, the town had a population of 500 and was connected to the outside world by a narrow-gauge railroad. But in 1888, a silver mine was discovered in a valley on the Coeur d'Alene River. The valley was a short, narrow canyon of the south fork. Burke had grown up northeast of Wallace along the banks of Canyon Creek, the south fork of the Coeur d'Alene River. The mine was called the Tiger Mine. The main streets of the town consisted of wooden buildings, most of them built over the river. Crowded wall to wall and tucked into the steep-sided narrow canyons with mine entrances perched on the steep slopes above, the railroad ran down the canyon between the buildings. The narrow main street was one loud noise coming from one saloon merging into the next. Burke had twenty-two drinking establishments lining both sides of that narrow dirty street that was also the railroad bed. Burke was a town that Marguerite described to her mother as one with "so many stories, and all of them true."

The canyon that held Burke was so deep that the sun could reach the town for only three hours a day in the winter. It was so narrow that the town's only street had to carry wagons and two railroads. The creek was a dump, and when it overflowed it took all the garbage downriver, and the main street became a creek bottom and a garbage heap in the overflow. Every time the freight train came through on the Northern Pacific tracks, it ran down the middle of the street and straight through the center of the Tiger Hotel.

The four-story Tiger Hotel was originally built as a boarding house for the Tiger Poorman Mines. It had one hundred fifty rooms and a beanery that served twelve hundred meals a day to the miners. The hotel had burned down in a grease fire in 1896 but had been rebuilt. The railroad tracks had been built through the hotel in 1906 when Harry Day of the Hercules Mine convinced the Northern Pacific to construct a spur track up to his loading platforms below Gorge Gulch. The hotel covered the whole canyon floor on which the railroad needed to build. The Federal Mining and Smelting Company, which owned the Tiger Poorman and its hotel, agreed to Day's request, providing that the portion of the hotel under which the railroad would pass be lined with sheet or corrugated iron as fire protection.

Marguerite and Amy were given a small cottage on the hillside just above the school. The school was big, and it had a great principal. Amy was assigned to the first grade, and Marguerite taught a fifth/sixth-grade combination. The young women were given a choice: They could cook for themselves, or they could go down to the hotel and eat at the beanery. Often they would choose the latter.

Eating at the beanery was interesting. Here were two pretty young teachers and twelve hundred single miners, most of whom were very shy. If you caught them looking at you, as soon as you looked back they would quickly look away and almost put their face in their plate.

Marguerite did notice one young man looking at her one day.

"I think someone has an eye on you," Amy said.

"Yes, Amy, twenty-four hundred eyes."

"No, the one over at the far table. He is much cleaner than the rest."

"Oh, be quiet, Amy."

It took about a month before the man finally walked over to Marguerite and Amy and introduced himself. "I'm William Franks. All my friends call me W.T. for short. I'm an electrician here at the mines. Been here about a year after getting out of the Navy."

"I'm Marguerite, and this is Amy. We teach at the school."

Marguerite found herself eating more and more at the beanery, and she and Amy began to sit with W.T. Marguerite gave W.T. a new nickname. W.T. always wore clean and perfectly pressed corduroy pants, and they could hear his legs rubbing before he reached their table. So his new name became C.L., short for "Corduroy Legs."

W.T., the son of a railroad engineer, was born in Colorado. He had studied electrical engineering at Stanford University in California and then had joined the Navy in California. He had been stationed on a submarine near the Panama Canal. When he took his discharge in California, he applied to work at the mines in San Francisco. That was how he had become a mining electrician in Burke, Idaho. Marguerite wrote to her mother that she had met someone she liked very much.

Marguerite spent two years in Burke, and she and W.T. became very close. The family had planned to spend the summer of 1920 back in Montana, and Amy was invited to go with them. W.T. was offered a position with the mining company in Haverhill, Massachusetts. He would be in training and would receive a salary for about fourteen months. On his way to Massachusetts, he stopped in Montana and spent a week with Marguerite's family. During his visit, he had trouble getting Marguerite away from the group so he could speak with her privately.

Amy was all over Marguerite. "I think he is serious," she teased. "This is it."

The teasing went on and on. Two days before he was to leave, he and Marguerite took a long walk. W.T. held both her hands, looked at her, and said, "Marguerite, I love you, and I want you to marry me. You know I will be gone for a while, but I will write you everyday."

"W.T., I do love you and would be honored to be your wife."

Their engagement was announced at dinner that night. It didn't seem to be much of a surprise. W.T. had talked to Joseph before dinner, and he had previously spoken with Mary. Joseph and Mary both liked W.T. a great deal. They could see his genuine affection for their daughter, and they could also see that he was a serious and hard worker and would take good care of a family. Marguerite and W.T. decided they would be married in the summer of 1921. It was hard for Marguerite to say good-bye to W.T.

That same summer, Leo graduated from the Colorado School of Mines and accepted a position as a design engineer for Anaconda Copper Company in Chile. He had already spent his summers working for the company in Montana.

Marguerite left for Burke in the fall. Mary liked having her daughter teaching so close to home. She could go up for visits, and Marguerite would come down for holidays.

W.T. kept his promise. He wrote Marguerite a letter every single day. Around Christmas, he wrote to tell her he had become a Catholic. He had taken instructions and had been attending services with his family back in Massachusetts. It was a surprise to Marguerite, who had never put pressure on him about his religious beliefs. Marguerite knew he was a good man, whatever his religion was. Mary was pleased, though. She said, "It is much easier if you go to the same church, that is, if you both go to church."

Marguerite decided to leave Burke and take a position in

Moravia, Idaho, so that she could more easily get home for weekends and holidays. She explained to her family her reason for teaching there rather than in Spokane. It seemed that Idaho didn't have a teacher's school and relied on teachers from Washington. As a result, many positions were available in Idaho at better pay.

In the summer, W.T. wrote that his father's health was failing and asked if they could be married in November so that his parents could attend. W.T. said that he would be back in late September to take up his job in Burke. It was hard for Marguerite to write and tell W.T. that she had taken a job in Moravia. Marguerite informed W.T. that it would not be a problem for her to plan a Thanksgiving wedding.

W.T.'s parents were selling their home in Colorado and moving to Visalia, California, where his sister and her husband were living. But W.T.'s father's health was failing fast.

Mary was very excited planning for Marguerite's wedding. It would be a small wedding for family and close friends only. When W.T. returned, he and Marguerite would go to Spokane to help Mary and Joseph plan the wedding. The guests would all be put up at the Davenport Hotel.

The wedding would be held at 7:30 a.m., followed by a breakfast at the hotel and a large Thanksgiving dinner at Mary and Joseph's house. Joseph arranged with a local bakery to cook the turkeys.

As the time grew closer, Mary was very busy. She was lucky to have Emma to help her, and Emma's daughter Ursula was quiet and easy to have around—she would sit for hours and play by herself.

CHAPTER FIFTEEN

THE DAY ARRIVED, and everyone got up early so as to be at church by 7:30 in the morning. Merlin was to be best man, since Leo couldn't make it back from Chile. Marguerite's old friend, Margaret Reilly, was maid of honor. As the vows were completed and she saw how happy her daughter looked, Mary held back tears while Joseph squeezed her hand.

At breakfast, everyone got to meet W.T.'s parents, Charles and Ida Franks, for the first time. Even though he was sick, Charles was easy to get to know. W.T.'s mother, Ida, was a very proper lady who showed that she had money, but she also had a way of making people feel relaxed around her.

After breakfast, they all went to the Gumps' house, where the guests were allowed to relax and get to know each other before the big dinner at 4 p.m. After dinner, Marguerite and W.T. slipped away from the crowd. They were to spend three days at the Davenport Hotel before W.T. had to go back to Burke and Marguerite to Moravia, which was right between Spokane and Burke.

That evening, Mary and Ida got to know each other a bit, and Mary promised to show Ida around Spokane. Joseph enjoyed Charles, who had retired from being a railroad engineer after being stationed in Grand Junction, Colorado. The many years of being jostled in the engine had affected his health, and the Franks family was now moving to California. Charles Franks had purchased a small orange grove near Visalia, California, to be near their daughter Levita and her husband, Had. He knew a lot about farming, a common topic of conversation between him and Joseph.

The Franks family stayed for about a week, and the two families spent a lot of time together. Joseph took the Franks family to the train when they left for California. Since Charles had worked for and retired from the railroad, he had a lifetime pass and had his own beautiful private compartment on the train.

W.T. came down to Spokane for Christmas. Since he had to return to Burke the day after Christmas and Marguerite still had some time before school started. Mary and Marguerite went back with him. It was fun for Marguerite to see all her old friends. A big dance was held on New Year's Eve. W.T. and Marguerite danced almost every dance. Mary didn't miss a dance, either. They didn't get home until 3:30 a.m. and had to get up early so Marguerite could get back to Moravia. When Marguerite returned to school, it was a lot easier, as they had hired a new teacher who took over the top four grades, leaving Marguerite the younger ones.

W.T. would visit Spokane one weekend, and Marguerite would visit W.T. the next. "The two of you are going to wear out those railroad tracks," Mary laughed.

"Mother, you and Dad didn't have to live apart right after you got married. You would have done the same thing."

"True," Mary agreed.

In early February, Marguerite realized she was pregnant, which pleased Mary. As soon as school was out, Marguerite returned to Spokane. In the meantime, W.T. had been offered a position with the Washington Water and Power Company in Spokane. Mary was happy to have Marguerite back in town. Marguerite and W.T. had rented a small apartment near Mary and Joseph. W.T. purchased a small crib on wheels for the baby.

With W.T. at work and Joseph's long hours, mother and daughter had lots of time together. Emma would come over, and all three of them would sew baby clothes. Mary was enjoying the pregnancy as much as Marguerite was. "This is going to be one spoiled child with all these women around."

"No, mother, he won't be spoiled."

"He—are you sure?" Mary asked.

"Yes. It will be a boy. W.T. wants to name him after his father—Charles Edward."

On September 13, when labor began, Marguerite went into the hospital. Her mother, her father, and W.T. were all with her. Marguerite had a hard time with the birth, and W.T. paced the hall, saying, "If she has this much trouble and this much pain, we'll never have another one."

Mary took his hand. "W.T., can we hold you to that? Please, relax."

After a difficult delivery, the baby was born on September 14, 1921. The doctor announced to W.T., "Marguerite had a hard time, but you have a big, healthy son."

Marguerite stayed in the hospital for ten days, and when she went home, Mary stayed with her for another week. At that time, women were required to stay in the hospital for ten days, with at least a week of rest at home. When Marguerite was released from the hospital, W.T. was required to pay the hospital bill—a total of sixty dollars for ten days.

It was a happy though crowded apartment with the baby, and after a year, W.T. and Marguerite started house hunting.

They found a house in an area called Manito Park. The home needed a lot of work, which W.T., with the help of Joseph, enjoyed doing. Mary and Marguerite kept busy making things for inside the house.

That winter, Mary caught pneumonia again, which was having an effect on her heart, and it took longer for her to recover. Charles was her pride and joy. Mary took him everywhere and had him talking at a very young age. Charles would put her face in his hands and say, "My dearie," which made Mary absolutely melt. Charles could have anything he wanted.

On October 23, 1923, a second son was born to W.T. and Marguerite. "W.T., do you remember your promise after Charles—no more? What happened?" Mary inquired.

"You know your daughter. She wants half a dozen, and she is hard to refuse."

"W.T., that isn't nice," Mary said, smiling.

Joseph, named after Marguerite's father, weighed only six pounds. He was so small that he slept in a chair near the stove where it was warm. Mary spent a lot of time with Marguerite helping with the children. It was easy, since Joseph had to stay at the firehouse for two or three days at a time. Mary was the best and proudest grandmother and would do anything for and give anything to those grandchildren.

Mary would sit at the window or on the porch and watch Charles work in the yard with his father. They even purchased him a little wheelbarrow. When Marguerite became pregnant again, Mary was concerned and hoped it would be a girl and that would be it.

One time when Mary was at the house, Joseph was crawling around the kitchen. No one saw him pick up one of his father's shoes and throw it into the oven. Later, Marguerite shut the oven door and turned on the oven. All of a sudden, she exclaimed, "What's that smell!" Mary immediately opened the oven and discovered the shoe, which she quickly pulled from the oven and took outside to cool off. When W.T. came home, he was furious, because the shoes were new. He had hard feet to fit, and these were very expensive ones. Charles stood beside his father with his hand on his hips looking at the shoe. "Daddy, you can fix it, you're a good electricianer." It was hard to stay mad at Charles, and everyone had a good laugh.

Mary went to the hospital with W.T. when the third child was born. When the doctor announced that Marguerite had had another son, Mary just looked at the doctor and said, "I sure wish it was a girl."

The doctor looked back and asked her, "Shall I put him back?"

W.T. was so excited. "It is hard to believe I have three sons." The baby was born February 26, 1925, and was baptized John David Franks.

Joseph worried a great deal about Mary's health, so he went to California to look for a job. He found one with Shell Oil Company, painting service stations. He purchased a small house in Sacramento and then asked Mary to join him.

Marguerite asked W.T. whether he would think about going to California if her mother went, but W.T. explained to her that he had a good job where they were and it would be difficult to leave. He did, however, send resumes to several companies in California.

Then Marguerite learned that she was pregnant again. Mary had been living with W.T. and Marguerite since Joseph had gone to California. W.T. started looking for a larger house, which he soon found. It was hard for the family to leave their small dollhouse that had been home for so long with its beautiful garden of flowers and vegetables, but they needed a larger home.

On August 26, 1926, a fourth son, Steven Robert, was born. (Mary couldn't believe that her daughter now had four sons.) When Steven Robert was only a couple of months old, Mary packed up and moved to California. Within another month, W.T. was offered a job in Oakland, California, with Pacific Gas and Electric Company (PG&E). He accepted the job, and the family sold the house and moved to California.

Charles had gone to California with Mary. He was five years old and wanted to be with his "dearie." It had made it a lot easier on Marguerite to have only the three boys.

Mary and Marguerite would be only eighty-five miles apart, which was still too far apart for both of them. Mary spent a lot of time in Oakland, helping Marguerite with her four boys.

Marguerite and W.T. found a small house near a park just behind an Italian grocery store. Mary often took the children to the park to play. Jack was the hard one to watch, as he liked to wander off. Mary had told Marguerite to tie a small rope around his waist while he was in the yard so that he could still wander without getting too far way. But no matter where he was, Jack was always busy getting into something. One day, the women noticed that Jack had stretched his rope to the limit. Jack was lying on his stomach, reaching under the fence for a mud puddle. He was able to get his hand into the mud, bring his hand back, and rub the mud all over himself. Mary and Marguerite both found this ritual amusing.

Another time, the children found a box of salamis that had been delivered to the grocery store and left out back. The children made a train of salamis all around the backyard. Neither Mary nor Marguerite had ever seen a salami before and thought they were mildewed sausages that had been discarded. The owner of the grocery store was very angry. "Do you know how much salami costs? It is a treat. Keep them kids out from behind my store."

It was funny watching the store owner collect the train of salamis. When W.T. came home, they couldn't wait to tell him the salami story, which he got a good laugh over. "That store owner will get over it. We buy enough from him."

The family had been in Oakland for just a little over a year when W.T. was transferred to a PG&E substation in Nicols, California. Nicols was out in the middle of nowhere, and Marguerite missed her park in Oakland. Once again, Marguerite and Mary would be a long distance from each other. Mary still found every excuse to spend time with her daughter and grandchildren. Joseph would complain with a smile, saying he was going back to Montana to find a replacement wife for Mary. Mary would tell him to go ahead and try to find one as good as she was.

Joseph was transferred by Shell to Santa Cruz, California, a small coastal town seventy-five miles south of San Francisco. Mary liked Santa Cruz, but Joseph was on the road a lot, and Mary didn't have Marguerite and the children to keep her busy. Soon after Marguerite and W.T. had moved to Nichols, Marguerite wrote Mary telling her that she was pregnant again. She wanted Mary to come and help her as her due date—December or January—approached.

Although it was only June, Marguerite wanted her mother to start preparing Joseph for her being gone again to help her with the new baby and the other children.

Mary told Marguerite that she would be there, but since this was the summer of 1928, she wanted to take Marguerite and the children to Spokane to visit Emma and her family. Mary would drive so that they could take their time and enjoy the trip. Mary picked up her family, and with a few tips from both W.T and Joseph, they headed for Spokane. The trip took two and a half days, with many toilet stops along the way. The children enjoyed the trip.

Emma and Collier hadn't seen the children in a couple of years. They were surprised that Marguerite was pregnant again but hoped she would have a girl at last.

Emma was worried about Mary, who had lost weight and was having trouble breathing. Emma asked Mary what the doctor had to say.

"My heart is tired," Mary responded, "and it has to work hard when I have asthma attacks. But there isn't much I can do."

Mary in turn was worried about Emma, who had also lost a lot of weight, but Emma assured Mary that she was feeling just fine.

It was a good visit for Mary, who missed Emma and their talks. The two women had been together for so long. Mary tried to talk Emma and her family into coming to California, but Collier wouldn't leave his job; Spokane was their home. Despite Mary's disappointment, the families had a good visit. Mary knew it was important for the children to remember their Aunt Emma.

Right after Christmas, Mary went to stay with Marguerite and help with the children when the new baby arrived. On January 2, 1929, the doctor delivered at their Nichols home a daughter, Mary Lee Franks. Mary told Marguerite, "Now that you have a daughter, you can quit."

Since Nichols was such a small community, everyone was friends. One neighbor had seven children who were the same ages as Marguerite's children. When Mary Lee was born, the neighbors all brought food and were there to help. Mary enjoyed the close community, and it took an adamant letter from Joseph to get her to come home to Santa Cruz.

Just after Mary returned to Santa Cruz, PG&E moved W.T. to Angel's Camp. The job was a promotion, and the Franks family would have a bigger house for the children. Angel's Camp was a beautiful area, and the children could go anywhere and be safe. The only problem was a family nearby who used the worst language Marguerite had ever heard. One night at dinner, Charles looked up and said, "Pass that son of a bitch butter." W.T. nearly fell out of his chair, and Marguerite had to leave the room because she couldn't keep from laughing. W.T. informed Charles, "You say, please pass the butter, and we will not have any more of that language. Is that understood?"

"Yes, sir," Charles replied.

Marguerite would write to her mother and tell her about her children's escapades. One day, the children were playing in the field in back of their house when they found a large box. The box was humming, and they assumed it was a transformer. They decided that something should be done, and one of them came up with a solution: "Let's kick it over." The "transformer" was a beehive, and out swarmed the bees, and off ran the children.

Steve, being the youngest, got turned around and ran the wrong way. The bees attached themselves to him. Marguerite could hear the poor little guy yelling as the bees stung him all over. She ran outside and covered him, carried him into the house, killed the bees, and picked out all the stingers. Steve's head and face were one big bump. Marguerite then made a baking soda paste, which she spread all over her sobbing and hurting son's body.

Another time, Marguerite wrote Mary about how Steve and Mary Lee had been playing in a field across the road and had found an abandoned outhouse. The children had put a board through the open door and up over the toilet and were running up and down the board. If they had fallen into the hole, no one would have known, and no one would have been able to find them. W.T. marched right over, knocked down the building, and filled in the holes.

Mary worried about Marguerite, though she did enjoy her letters about her busy children.

On one trip to Santa Cruz, Marguerite and W.T. found a small house on an acre of land and found a way to buy it as a summer home. Mary was so excited about their purchase. It was a funny red house, but it would make a great summer home. The house was in East Santa Cruz near DeLaveaga Park and not far from the beach. Joseph offered to work on the house and take care of it for the family.

Mary and Joseph went up to Angel's Camp for the frog-jumping contest, of which Angel's Camp was the home. Jack was excited. He had caught a large frog, and his father had entered him into the contest. Jack fed the frog and kept it warm behind the stove in a cage. Everyone was waiting for the big day. Jack was sure he would win with his frog. On that day, Jack took his frog out to the contest. The frog, however, had had such a good life just eating and sleeping behind the stove, that it wouldn't even jump. It just sat there with its eyes shut. No matter what they did, the frog wouldn't jump. Soon everyone started laughing while poor Jack sat next to his frog and began to cry. W.T. put his arm around Jack. "It's okay," he consoled his son. "He may not jump, but he is the fattest and best-looking frog around. Let's take him home." Jack picked up his frog and put it in his shirt. "It's okay, frog, I still love you."

Mary and Joseph stayed to help the family move to a new home on the other side of Angel's Camp. The house was bigger, with a garden and a fenced yard. Next door lived a couple with a large garden and many fruit trees who were happy to have a large family to share their harvest with. Mary and Marguerite canned the surplus. W.T. would come home and ask, "Is this my home or a cannery?"

It became more difficult each time Mary returned to Santa Cruz, since Mary and Marguerite enjoyed so many things together.

Mary received another letter from Marguerite, who was very angry and had been to Charles' school taking on the principal. Charles was a good student and was usually very well-behaved, but one day he had written a love note to a girl he liked at school. The principal had taken the note and made Charles read it in every classroom in the school. Charles had come home totally humiliated and didn't want to go back to school. Marguerite went right over and told the principal that he should be fired, that he was sadistic and a poor example for children. She told him that she was going to the school board over this. The principal admitted that he had used poor judgement and said that he would apologize to Charles. Marguerite told him that it was a little late, since all the children were already teasing him. Just reading the letter made Mary angry. No one picked on her Charles! It was a good thing she hadn't been there, or she would probably have hit the principal with a chair.

During the fall of 1931, things started to look bad. A depression had started with the stock market collapse in October 1929, even though the people had been given repeated assurances from high authorities, both in government and in finance, that prosperity was just around the corner. W.T. and Marguerite felt that they were all right, since everyone still needed power, and W.T. assumed that his job was secure. After the market failure, agriculture started to slow down. Farmers had overproduced. Prices started to fall, and farm purchases declined. Then it hit—industrial overexpansion. The American industrial plant had been overbuilt during the period of the boom, and now everyone was cutting back. W.T. was laid off from his job. He and Marguerite decided that it would be best if they moved to Santa Cruz to their summer home.

W.T. rented a truck, and the move was started. It took one truck alone to move all the canned goods Marguerite and her mother had canned. Mary and Joseph helped them move into their house. Joseph built shelves in the garage for the canned goods. He and W.T. built a barn and purchased a milk cow. With a home and small savings, the family was better off than many others.

The house was small, and plans to add a room and put on a larger garage were drawn up. First priority, however, was finding a job and getting the children in school. It was the first time that a Catholic school was available to the family, and Mary put the children in Holy Cross Grammar School, run by the Sisters of Charity from San Francisco.

Times were hard on W.T. A college graduate and trained electrician, W.T. could find only odd jobs digging bulbs for a flower grower or working at a sand pit. But the family had plenty of food with their own garden, cow, pigs, and chickens.

After W.T. and Marguerite's savings ran out, Mary and Joseph tried to help, but Joseph had also lost his job. The worst thing for Marguerite and W.T. was not being able to pay their mortgage. A notice was put on the house that it was to be sold at auction in ten days. W.T. sent a telegram to President Roosevelt, who had promised that "no American would lose his home." Within a week, the house was refinanced with a government loan, and the home was saved.

Mary would always say, "Our family has always admired President Roosevelt for what he did for my daughter."

Joseph just couldn't make it in Santa Cruz. He was offered a job at the Buffalo Brewery in Sacramento, a job he couldn't refuse. Once again, Mary would be separated from Marguerite and the children, but it was necessary.

As soon as Joseph was settled in Sacramento he was able to trade his Santa Cruz home for an acre of land right next to W.T. and Marguerite's property. He figured he could build his retirement home there.

The first winter Mary and Joseph were in Sacramento, they received a letter from W.T. saying that Marguerite had caught pneumonia. Mary returned to Santa Cruz to help. Marguerite became very sick and had to be hospitalized. The doctors discovered that she was pregnant and that the pneumonia had started an infection in her lungs. They knew that Marguerite would lose the baby, and they didn't think she would survive, either. They operated to remove a rib and placed a drainage tube in her back. Mary sat with Marguerite for hours telling her, "You must live, you have five children who need you. You must live."

Father McGrath from Holy Cross came to the hospital and gave Marguerite her last rites of the church. Mary's health wasn't the best anymore, but she took over caring for Marguerite's family. She would go out in the backyard and cry and pray for Marguerite. "She must live."

Marguerite was in critical condition for almost four months. Finally, she began to show small signs of improvement. The doctors told W.T. and Mary, "If she should live, she will be an invalid the rest of her life."

After five months, Marguerite was allowed to go home as long as she had home care. No one could believe how fast she began to recover, and by May, Mary was able to return to Sacramento.

Joseph enjoyed his work with the Buffalo Brewery, and he had started a cleaning company on the side called Spic and Span. With the extra money, he was able to help Marguerite in Santa Cruz.

Sometimes Joseph was afraid he would lose both Mary and Marguerite. He could see Mary's health going down slowly. It was getting harder for Mary to breathe, and now Marguerite was so sick. Then things started to improve some. The government started the WPA (a work assistance program), and W.T. was hired to work on Highway 17, a road over the mountains between Santa Cruz and Los Gatos. He worked at the sand plant, which provided the sand for the cement.

Mary would still come down to Santa Cruz to be with Marguerite, who had remarkably regained her health.

Friends of the family had separated and asked if their daughter Bonnie could stay with Marguerite's family. This girl was the same age as Mary Lee and the couple offered to pay for her room and board. Bonnie came to live with the Franks family, who found the extra money to be a big help.

During Marguerite's recovery, the doctor, Samuel Randall, kept a close eye on her. He told her that since she had lost the previous baby, she couldn't have any more children. He also told her that "five was enough."

Mary took over full running of Marguerite's house and taking care of her family. She was a great help to W.T. but a real worry to Joseph. Mary made the trip from Sacramento to Santa Cruz many times. She would go to Sacramento and get Joseph settled and happy, then head for Santa Cruz to be with Marguerite and her family. Joseph would say to her, "Mary, you are going to kill yourself. Your health isn't that good."

"But Joseph, if I keep busy, I don't think about myself. You know I love you, but I feel I must help Marguerite."

Mary's protection of Marguerite was her passion. Mary felt that she must be there to protect her family at all costs, even if it meant losing her own life. Joseph believed that her need to help had something to do with the time she had been at the mission. Mary would do anything to keep and protect her family.

Mary and Joseph came to Santa Cruz for Christmas 1933. Joseph brought W.T. a couple of cases of Buffalo beer. It was a treat to have beer in the house.

Christmas morning was beautiful. Joseph had made blocks, which he had painted different colors for the children. W.T. had made a table and chairs. So many homemade gifts! Dinner was a banquet—a large turkey that they had raised, with potatoes and gravy and all the trimmings.

Marguerite announced that she was pregnant and the baby was due in August. There was total silence. Finally, Mary asked, "Marguerite, what did the doctor say?"

"He said he didn't believe it, but that I'm healthy enough to carry the baby."

As soon as Mary and Joseph returned to Sacramento, Mary started to put pressure on Joseph to move back to Santa Cruz. Joseph told Mary, "There is no way I can make a living in Santa Cruz. I'm very lucky to have a job—a good job."

"But Joseph, I must be close to Marguerite, especially now. This will be her sixth baby. I must help if I can."

"Mary, your health isn't good. Your heart is getting weak. You must take care of yourself."

"Merlin is no good and a wanderer. We never know where he is. Leo is in the Philippines with Edna, and except for last year, we haven't seen him in eight years. I have only Marguerite. She is my daughter, my friend, and she is so good to me."

"Mary, you will be no good to her if you die. You must take care of yourself. Please, for me?"

Mary did wait until a month before the baby was due to go to Santa Cruz. She loved being around the children. Her favorite was still Charles, who was now almost thirteen years old. Charles was such a handsome young man. To make extra money, he raised turkeys in a large pen out by the barn.

Marguerite and W.T. decided that this baby would be born at home. As the due date drew closer, the downstairs bedroom was readied. On August 12, 1934, a daughter, Rita Joan, was born. Dr. Randall was proud and told everyone that the baby was a very healthy girl and that he was amazed that Marguerite was just fine.

Mary stayed until October, then returned to Sacramento. "Joseph, I can't help it, it is so hard to leave Santa Cruz."

During the fall of 1935, Mary had a hard time. The doctor said the asthma was taxing her heart and she must be careful. Mary wrote to Marguerite to tell her she was feeling good though her health was failing. Marguerite wanted her mother near her so they could support each other. Mary asked Joseph, "Please, Joseph, retire. I want to move back to Santa Cruz. I know I'm dying, and I want to be around my family. Please, Joseph."

Joseph's pension from the Buffalo Brewery would be small, but with his Social Security check, he would be okay. He put in for his retirement. Mary went ahead to Santa Cruz and found a small apartment not far from the Franks home on Fairmount Avenue. Joseph did all the packing and left Sacramento in March of 1936.

Marguerite could see her mother's health starting to go faster. She took Mary in to see Dr. Randall. Marguerite stayed back to talk to the doctor. "Please, doctor, how is my mother?"

"Marguerite, I don't think she will live another year. Her heart is enlarged and is missing beats. She will just get weaker and weaker, then finally go into a coma and die."

"But Doctor, she does so much and seems to have energy."

"She is pushing herself hard, which isn't good. But let her be happy."

In November, Mary and Joseph moved in with W.T. and Marguerite so that Mary and Marguerite could help each other. The two did offer each other support, since Marguerite was now getting bigger with her seventh child.

When summer came, the canning started, but the big job was helping to kill and clean Charles' turkeys.

Marguerite went into labor the last day of August, and at 6 p.m. on September 1, 1936, a son was born at home in the downstairs bedroom. W.T. was milking the cows when he was given the news. "That's it. No more, a son to start and a son to end. No more." The boy was baptized James Albert and his godparents were the Murphys, who lived nearby.

By December 1936, Mary was required to spend more and more time in bed, but she got a burst of energy around Christmas. She and Marguerite baked one hundred dozen cookies to make gift plates for friends.

Charles saved a big turkey for Christmas, and it had to be taken to the bakery to be cooked.

Mary seemed to know it was going to be her last Christmas. She had knit sweaters for all the children, and Joseph felt that they would go broke with her spending for presents. But he wanted her to be happy.

W.T. and the boys went out into the hills to cut a Christmas tree. The tree was so big that they cut off the bottom and top and put the middle in the room. The kids were so excited. "What a great tree! It looks like it goes right through the roof."

The whole family went to midnight mass at Holy Cross. The church was always beautiful, with the Christmas decorations and the manger scene. Christmas morning was beautiful. Mary seemed to be having as much fun as the children.

"W.T., Marguerite, you have a wonderful family. I'm glad to be a part of it." The children loved "Grandma Mary," or "Dearie," as she was called.

The family had a small New Year's Eve party, and the children were allowed to stay up. At midnight, they all went outside and beat on pans with wooden spoons. Joseph recalled a night in Montana long ago. "Mary, do you remember our first New Year's Eve on our farm, when you worried about Emma and me breaking your wooden spoons?"

Mary remembered. "Yes, I do. And you promised me you'd replace them. But you never broke one spoon."

Joseph hugged his wife, who seemed so frail to him now. They had hot apple cider to start 1937.

The New Year wasn't good for Mary. Although she could do less and less, she was a great help to Marguerite, since she took almost total care of the baby, Jimmy. Mary would sit in a rocking chair in the living room, feeding and rocking the baby. Marguerite would tell Mary, "That baby is getting more attention than all the other children put together."

Marguerite would sit with her mother for hours talking about her childhood. Mary was pleased that her daughter remembered so many things about when she was young. For all these years, it had been hard for Mary to think back on her own parents and the first eighteen years of her life, but now she thought it was the time. She thought of her wonderful mother, who had taught her some of the ways of her people, and she thought of her father, James, and now she was holding a new life with the same name, all connected through her. Her life made her glad.

Joseph helped around the farm. He took care of the cows, pigs, and chickens. He had painted the entire outside of the house white and would tell Marguerite, "I'm happy if I'm busy, but I don't know what I will do if I lose Mary. She is my life."

As Mary grew weaker, it became harder for her to do anything. If she was in bed, she became congested and would have trouble breathing. If she sat up, she would become very tired. The doctor had told Marguerite that she should keep her walking, or else her lungs would fill with fluid.

By the first of June, Mary could hardly breathe and was suffering. The doctor was called in again. After examining Mary, he spoke with Joseph and Marguerite. "She has a strong body, but the heart just can't do its job anymore. She is slowly drowning as her lungs fill, and her heart can't pump them clear. Eventually her heart will quit."

Mary died on June 22, 1937, with her family at her side. It was very hard on Marguerite, who had lost not only her mother but also her best friend.

Joseph purchased a plot at the Holy Cross cemetery for the two of them. He would miss his Mary.

Mary had come a long way, from a girl who was called a half-breed in Montana to a proud mother and grandmother. She was a good, gentle person who would always be "Dearie" to her grandchildren.

Her cherished physical possessions still exist: her painting, the silver button-hole maker, and the three silver napkin rings. Her greatest treasure shone from her—the love she received from her parents, Maggie and James Wells, from Miss Fields her beloved friend, and from Joseph her devoted husband. This love she passed on to her children and grandchildren. Her love will live on in her family, although that precious A'a'ninin tradition is gone forever.

EPILOGUE

Of Mary and Joseph's children:

Merlin died a young man on one of his "wandering trips" in Salt Lake City.

Leo, who married Edna Hayes, was a Design Engineer for Haussermann Enterprises in the Phillippines in 1934. They had a daughter born May 10, 1937 named Marguerite after Leo's sister. She only lived a few days and died from spina bifida.

On January 2, 1942, Edna was taken prisoner by the Japanese and placed in Santo Tomas. Leo was taken prisoner in the Southern part of the Phillippines (Davao). He was later moved back to Manila.

In 1945, General Yamashita, the overall Japanese Commander, declared Manila an "open" city. Rear Admiral Iwabuchi, ignoring the order, went on a rampage of destruction, devastation, atrocity, rape, and pillage. He killed over 100,000 people in Manila including Leo Joseph Gump.

His wife Edna survived Santo Tomas and returned to the United States. She practiced nursing in Sacramento, CA until her death August 9, 1987.

Marguerite remained in Santa Cruz, California until her death on April 21, 1991.

Of her eight children, three are deceased: William Joseph, John David, and Vincent Edward.

Five children still survive: Charles Edward, Stephen Robert, MaryLee Wright, Rita Boehner and James Albert.

Marguerite and William had 32 grandchildren, 44 great-grand-children, and 7 great-great-grandchildren.

The original home at 719 Fairmount Ave. is still in the family and owned and lived in by James Albert Franks.

BIBLIOGRAPHY

Banks, Eleanor. *Wandersong*. Caxton Printers, 1950.

Bruchac, Joseph. *The Native American Sweat Lodge*. Crossing Press, 1993.

Burlingame, Merrill G. *The Montana Frontier*. Big Sky Books, 1980.

Cody, William F. and Henry Inman. *The Great Salt Lake Trail*. Macmillan, 1898.

Cooper, John M. *The Gros Ventres of Montana: Part II, Religion and Ritual*. The Catholic University of America Press, 1975.

Costello, Gladys. "White Man Left His Name To A Mountain." *Phillips County News*, 1987.

"Death of James Wells." *The River Press*, Fort Benton, February 11, 1885.

Dixon, Dr. Joseph K. *The Vanishing Race—The Last Great Indian Council*.

Flannery, Regina. *The Gros Ventres of Montana: Part I, Social Life*. The Catholic University of America Press, 1975.

Fort Belknap Education Department. *Recollections of Fort Belknap's Past*. Fort Belknap Indian Community, 1982.

Fort Belknap Education Department. *War Stories of the White Clay People*. Fort Belknap Indian Community, 1982.

Fowler, Loretta. *Shared Symbols, Contested Meanings: Gros Ventre Culture and History, 1778-1984*. Cornell University Press, 1987.

Hardin, Floyd. *Campfires and Cowchips*. Floyd Hardin, 1972.

"Historic Building." *The River Press*, Fort Benton, December 13, 1989.

Horse Capture, George, editor. *The Seven Visions of Bull Lodge*. University of Nebraska Press, 1992.

Howard, Joseph Kinsey. *Montana: High, Wide, and Handsome*. University of Nebraska Press, 1983.

Jackson, W. Turrentine. *Wells Fargo Stagecoaching in Montana Territory*. Montana Historical Society Press, 1979.

Kroeber, A.L. *Ethnology of the Gros Ventres*. American Museum of Natural History, Anthropological Paper, vol. 1 part 4, 1908.

Lavender, David. *Let Me Be Free*. Harper Collins, 1992.

MacDonald, Henry. "A Pioneer." *The River Press*, Fort Benton, January 26, 1887.

Marshall, S.L.A. *Crimsoned Prairie: The Indian Wars*. Da Capo Press, 1972.

McBride, Genevieve. *The Bird Tail*. Vantage Press, 1974.

McHugh, Tom. *The Time of the Buffalo*. University of Nebraska Press, 1979.

Morgan, L.H. *The Indian Journal, 1859-1982*. University of Michigan Press, 1959.

Noyes, A.J. *In the Land of Chinook: The Story of Blaine County*. State Publishing Co., 1917.

Overholser, Joel. *Fort Benton: World's Innermost Port*. River Press, 1987.

Overholser, Joel. "James Wells Had Very Busy, Adventurous Life In Area." *The River Press*, Fort Benton, August 19, 1981.

Palladino, Laurence Benedict. *Indian & White In the Northwest: A History of Catholicity in Montana*. J. Murphy & Co., 1894.

Schoenberg, Wilfred. *Jesuits in Montana*. The Oregon Jesuit, 1960.

Toole, K. Ross. *Montana: An Uncommon Land*. University of

Oklahoma Press, 1943.

Utley, Robert M. *The Indian Frontier of the American West, 1846-1890*. University of New Mexico Press, 1987.

Vogel, Virgil J. *American Indian Medicine*. University of Oklahoma Press, 1990.

Washburn, Wilcomb E. *Red Man's Land/White Man's Law*. University of Oklahoma Press, 1995.

White, Jon Manchip. *Everyday Life of the North American Indians*. Dorset Press, 1979.

Willard, John. *Adventure Trails in Montana*. State Publishing Co., 1964.

Winther, Oscar Osburn. *Via Western Express & Stagecoach*. Stanford University Press, 1945.

UNPUBLISHED SOURCES

Bureau of Indian Affairs, Fort Belknap Reservation:
Office Files.

Montana Historical Society, Helena:
Papers of T.C. Power.

National Archives, Records of the Bureau of Indian Affairs, Washington, D.C.
Central Files, Fort Belknap Agency.
Indian Census Rolls, 1888-1911.